D0948826

A Mother's Guide to Manhood

Mother and Son
Dr. Gwen Spratt and Dalen Spratt

authorHOUSE®

AuthorHouse™
1663 Liberty Drive
Bloomington, IN 47403
www.authorhouse.com
Phone: 1-800-839-8640

First published by AuthorHouse 1/11/2011

ISBN: 978-1-4567-1377-5 (sc)
ISBN: 978-1-4567-1378-2 (e)
ISBN: 978-1-4567-1379-9 (dj)

Library of Congress Control Number: 2010918964

Printed in the United States of America

Dedication

To the countless women that have successfully taken on the role
of both mother and father, your efforts do not go unnoticed.

To my father, if it hadn't been for these circumstances, I would not
be the man I am today. Thank you for allowing us to tell OUR story.

And to you Mom, we did it. We weathered the storm.

Table of Contents

Introduction

The best teachers in life are those who have not only studied, but truly experienced the message that they are trying to relay. Whether it is religion, sports, or simple life lessons, your words and actions must be genuine. A wise man once told me, "You can't teach what you don't know, but if you do know, why not spread the knowledge."

The words on these pages were written to inspire hope. They are not only meant for the multitude of people that don't believe a woman can raise a son into a successful man without the immediate help of a father, but as well as for the individuals who are proving that theory wrong every day. There is hope, I am proof.

Through faith, strength, dedication, and prayer a former school teacher turned pastor was able to successfully raise her son into a respectable, focused, and driven man. This story and its lessons highlight the ups and downs, the smiles and frowns, and the tears of joy and sorrow that are all a part of the tremendous journey that a mother and son embark on together through life's everlasting trials and tribulations.

Gwen's Foreward

This book is written for every mother and son whose life is absent of a husband or father. For every mother who struggles daily to rear a son who someday will boldly say to her, "Mama, you did a good job with me."

The intent of this book is not to serve as a perfect model for child rearing because none of us are perfect. Instead, this book is written to share, encourage and offer support to all mothers and sons who believe or have been told a son cannot be successful in life without the daily guidance of a man.

- Dr. Gwen Spratt

Dalen's Foreward

To the naked eye my life would seem perfect and seamless. People look at the fact that my mother is a Pastor and my father is a Doctor and they automatically subconsciously compare me to a "Cosby-esque" television lifestyle, assuming that I am spoiled and can't fathom the hardships that life tends to throw at the average individual. The irony of the situation is that the same hardships that I have kept secret all my life have molded me into the individual I am today, and have allowed me to surpass the expectations of my fellow counterparts.

Throughout my life I have accomplished a plethora of achievements that I can only credit to God and my upbringing. My peers have always viewed me as a spoiled individual who has always had everything given to him and does not really know what it means to struggle or have hardships. If they only knew my story! From an early age I was taught the value of hard work by my mother. I watched over the years as my mother successfully transitioned from a 3rd grade school teacher to a Pastor of a thriving inner city church. Seeing my mother grow what was once a once-a-week Bible study into a fully functioning, operating church truly amazed and inspired me. That strong inspiration taught me the true value of independence and dedication. For her, I am forever grateful.

To a child, gifts and presents make the world go round; although these materialistic joys are an extreme highlight, the most important thing a family can ever offer an adolescent is stability. It is one thing to grow up with both parents being present, or even coming from a single parent household, but it is a whole different story when you have one consistently solid adult figure around and another that comes and goes as they please. The last scenario just does not leave any room for stability. With one parent acting as a revolving door, the child is left on a continuous emotional rollercoaster, left vulnerable and prone to disappointment on a consistent basis. The worst possible situation a parent could possibly find themselves in is having a child that has no hope. Parents must understand that children are not as naïve as they at times may seem. Contrary to popular belief, children do learn from their mistakes, even if that mistake is something as ordinary as putting their faith into a parent that constantly lets them down.

Growing up as my mother's only child and the youngest of my father's three children, I was forced to go out and make friends outside the household. These friends and their parents allowed me a glimpse into what I thought a real family truly was. With every opportunity that presented itself I was packing an overnight bag and escaping to a friend's home. I thought it was amazing to see a mother and a father sitting down at the dining table having dinner with the children. I found it astonishing that a father would actually take the time out his schedule to go outside and practice basketball with his son. It amused me to find myself amidst a real life father son conversation about the nature of girls. These simple everyday things seemed to be so far out of the norm for me. It was almost as if every time I left the confines of my home I entered into a world only seen on the Disney Chanel. Now, don't get me wrong, I am not saying that my friends and their families didn't have any problems, I am just speaking from a child's view point on how I perceived the situation as presented to me.

I can honestly say that through everything I have been through, God has truly blessed me with an excellent teammate in my mother. She was always able to provide me with the stability I needed as a growing young adolescent. She kept me fed, clothed, entertained, and wanting for nothing. She was and still is nothing less of a Saint in my book. Having her by my side made my life's matriculation one full of joy and happiness. It is truly a blessing to have my mother as a strong support system in my life; she always made it known that no matter the situation, she would be by my side, and for that I am grateful.

- Dalen L. Spratt

Lorenzo's Foreward

Men have often said that it takes a man, to raise a boy, into a man. The validity of the statement has always been and forever will be in question.

A Mother's Guide to Manhood addresses a Godly woman's effort to guide her son into manhood, while facing seemingly insurmountable odds and obstacles. In the mist of being married to a man who developed a raging poly-addiction, who was more not at home, than at home, a husband and father in absentia.

The fortitude, strength, long suffering, and love for God, son, husband, the church and its members, family, and many others, speaks of a remarkable woman who I greatly admire and love. My son who I am greatly pleased and so dearly love, admire and respect for responding to this God kind of love, maturing and growing up to be what his Heavenly Father desired for him to be, I am thankful.

It is the milieu of Gods' love that the fulfillment of His words which states, "Train up a child in the way he should go and he will not depart from it." Our Heavenly Father is always present to lead, guide, deliver, protect, and provide, while tutoring us, if we will let God fulfill his plan. For with God all things are possible; love and forgive.

I thank God daily for my wife, Gwen and son, Dalen for forgiving me and loving me.

- Lorenzo Spratt

Preamble

To fully know someone is to understand their past, present, and future wholeheartedly. However, this philosophy is only theoretically true because people walk around on a daily basis only allowing others a mere glimpse into their being. At first glance some individuals may seem to be perfectly well put together, but take a deeper look and realize that no one knows the full extent of their story. No one knows their journey, for it is the trials and tribulations of the past that build the character of the future. For as individuals we are all walking novels waiting for someone to go beyond the cover, past the intro, and read into the many chapters of our lives.

From the outside looking in, our lives seemed perfect. My mother was a pastor of a thriving inner city church and my father was a traveling emergency room physician. We lived in a wonderful suburban brick home with a huge backyard. What more could one possibly ask for, right?

As the sun began to set and doors began to lock around the neighborhood for the evenings, I knew in my heart other people were settling down for a quality family meal in the comforts of their own homes with those they loved the most. The same visions of sunsets and sounds of door locks held an entirely different meaning my mother and me. These everyday occurrences signified one thing and one thing only, the start of dissention.

What was perceived earlier as an end to a productive day for most, quickly turned into an outright battle zone within my household; the war between family and addiction began to quickly rage rapidly throughout the core of our home.

PART 1 – GWEN
A Dream Becomes a Nightmare

The Beginning

I am the eighth daughter in a family of nine girls raised in Jefferson, Texas. I was blessed to be raised by a very strong mother and father, both whom loved me and would do anything they could for my sisters and me. My father was often gone, so my mother became the cornerstone of our family. My mother prayed a lot and never failed to spare the rod, all the while keeping my sisters and me in school and in church. She was truly the head and we were the tail of the family, with that being said, I can honestly say that the tail had great respect for the head.

My parents raised their daughters to be strong black women, never weak and never needing someone to do things for us that we were well capable of doing ourselves. They taught us to be outspoken but respectful, while constantly instilling in us the value of work. In the midst of all their teachings, my parents remained very protective of us, as a result, my sisters and I have always exuded the same protective nature over our own children.

The First Marriage

I made the mistake of getting married at nineteen years of age. My first marriage caused me to meditate on the traits a husband or man should exemplify when it came to manhood and relationship building. I foolishly entered into a marriage with a man I thought I knew. This man, my husband, abused me both physically and mentally constantly. For the life of me, I still don't know why, till this day, I married at such a young age. I guess the old saying love is blind holds a lot of truth in most cases. My life with an insanely jealous and very insecure husband was hard to say the least. Amidst the struggle, violence, and depression, I was still able to balance working a full time job and pursuing a full time college degree. Being focused and driven were the only things that kept me sane during these trying days.

Those few years of marriage, to me, were almost like being dead. Finally I could not take any more abuse, I gathered enough courage was able to leave and divorce my husband with the help of my family and a special friend. Being focused on the goal I had set, I did, however earn my B.A. and Master's degrees in Early Childhood Education from the University of Minnesota before I left.

Fresh out of a detrimental marriage, I chose to remain single for a few years and work and just enjoy life to the fullest. After so many years of physical and mental abuse and I began to learn to value myself. Even throughout my past turmoil, I still looked at life through a clear glass rather than a cloudy one.

The Second Marriage

I never dreamed that October 15, 1980 would be the beginning of the rest of my life. To me it started off as a normal day. I woke up early, went to work, and talked to my sister several times that day, just as I always did. The only difference was instead of going home to spend a quiet night with my sister and niece I went home to prepare for something that I had never experienced before, a blind date.

My sister Fay was a well known beautician in Dallas. She had recently cut the hair of a new doctor who was from out of town, and of course with me on her mind, she asked him whether not he was married. When he answered "no," she told him about me and asked if he would be interested in meeting me. My sister Fay considered herself nothing less of a master matchmaker, and without my consent, Fay boldly informed the young doctor that I would go out with him. My mother always taught us to respect and obey our older sisters, since Fay was my elder; I had no choice in this matter

Who would have ever thought that one haircut could potentially predetermine the next 28 years of my life. What started off as one blind date seamlessly transitioned into that young doctor becoming my husband and the father of my only child. Within six months of meeting we had become inseparable. We were together constantly, friends and family would always tease us by saying it was as if we were conjoined at the hip. At the end of six months we decided to get married. Growing up as children, my sisters and I used to always play house. For some reason during our games I would always say that my husband was a doctor. I don't remember the day I stopped saying I wanted to marry a doctor and started saying, "I am going to *marry* a doctor," but all I know is my words became reality.

With the help of family and friends, within a week's time we successfully planned and organized a beautiful wedding and reception. And to add to my dream day, I was also able to have my wedding dress made specifically for me… The love and support shown that day was tremendous, my entire family including my mother and father attended the wedding.

Saturday, March 7, 1981, I cried all day. It was my wedding day, and I was overcome with a spirit of excitement. I was beyond happy and my lifelong dream was being realized, I had wanted to marry a doctor since I was six years old. My sisters kept asking why I was crying, but I couldn't give them an answer. Deep inside me there was a feeling that only my tears could answer. I believe to this very day my tears were trying to prepare me for the struggle, the fight, and the battle that lay ahead of me. The turmoil alone would cause me much pain and loneliness and take me to near financial ruin.

The Birth of Dalen

The first couple of years of my marriage were wonderful. I continued to work, we bought a new home, we shopped for furniture, and we took wonderful vacations to places I never thought I would ever have the opportunity to relax and enjoy. My husband's medical practice was thriving tremendously. Things couldn't have been more perfect for the both of us; we were seriously in a world all our own. The only thing missing for me at this point in my life was a child of my own. After serious discussion, my husband and I made the decision to have a baby. After months of disappointment we decided to have a complete fertility workup. After the workup was completed, I was given the most disappointing news of my life: I was told I would never be able to have a baby. My tubes were completely blocked and nothing could be done about it. At the time I accepted the doctor's report, yet part of me still longed to be a mother. I had twenty-plus nieces and nephews I loved dearly, and whose lives I was a big part of, but I still longed to have someone call me mama.

I went about living my life, working, loving my family and being the best wife I could be to my husband. Life was still good for me. As the days passed, the time my husband spent with me began to decrease, but I convinced myself that it was okay. A couple of years later, my body began to play tricks on me. I started having emotions I had never had before. I found myself crying for days on end with no apparent reason. My appetite began to change, I didn't have the faintest idea what the real problem was. One morning I told my husband I felt something was wrong with me. I told him I thought I had cancer, but for some reason my concerns didn't seem to alarm him, He just nonchalantly told me to see my doctor.

Before I could get in to see my doctor, one of my husband's friends from medical school came to visit with her new husband. Early that Saturday morning, Ada and I sat at the kitchen table drinking coffee and sharing small talk. At some point in our conversation I began to cry uncontrollably, so much that it startled Ada into asking me what was wrong. I told her I didn't know, but I knew something was seriously wrong with me. I told her about my appetite and crying spells. After listening to me pour my heart out with concerns, she looked at me, smiled and said, "Gwen, you are fine. There is nothing wrong with you other than that you are pregnant." I quickly said, "Oh no, I can't be pregnant. My tubes are completely blocked and the doctor said I would never be able to have children." Ada looked at me with those piercing eyes and said again, "Girl, you are going to have a baby." She suggested, just as my husband had done before, I contact my doctor as soon as possible to have some tests done to confirm my pregnancy.

Early Monday morning I called my doctor's office and told the receptionist I needed to come in as soon as possible because I thought I was pregnant. The receptionist put me on hold and the next voice I heard was that of my doctor's nurse. I relayed the same concern to her, and without hesitation, the nurse reminded me of my past test results and told me I couldn't possibly be pregnant. I persisted in my need to see the doctor, so finally she agreed to give me an appointment, and told me to be there the next day (Tuesday) at 2:00 p.m. I was up early the next day. I didn't want anyone to accompany me to the doctor's office; this was something I had to do alone. At this point my emotions were unbearable; I couldn't even control my thoughts because they were running relays throughout my head. I couldn't breathe as my heart began to beat faster and faster.

Finally, I arrived at my doctor's office, walking in with sweaty palms and all. I registered at the front desk and waited quietly until they called my name. After what seemed like an eternity, the nurse finally opened the door and beckoned for me to come. Although my eyes saw her motioning for me to follow her, it was as if I was stuck in a daze. I quickly snapped out of it, got up, grabbed my things and followed her into the exam room. As soon as we entered the room, she told me to undress from the waist down, and without hesitation I followed her instructions to the letter because I didn't want to irritate her. She didn't believe I was pregnant anyway and I didn't want to appear to be some kind of sicko. After I undressed from the waist down and draped myself with the sheet, the nurse came back in and asked me several questions that I answered as best I could. As she asked her questions, there was a little smile on her face. In my mind her sinister smile told me she thought I *was* in fact a sicko - one of those neurotic women who wants to be pregnant so badly they begin to experience symptoms of false pregnancy.

The wait for the doctor seemed to drag on and on but actually, it was only a few minutes. When the doctor entered the room, he looked at me and said, "So Gwen, why are you here today?" This was the same doctor who had done the complete fertility workup on me and given me the report of never being able to have a child on past occasions. You can only imagine the look he gave me when I told him I thought I was pregnant. Of course he didn't believe me, but because he was a doctor on staff at the same hospital as my husband, he suggested I take a urine test. I hopped off the exam table and went into the restroom and did as asked. I gave the sample to the nurse and was told to get dressed and wait for the results.

The wait seemed like a lifetime. Finally the doctor himself came in to get me and politely asked me to follow him. Usually I am able to read people's faces but for some reason I couldn't this time. The doctor just looked at me and asked me to follow him into his office. He walked around to his desk and told me to have a seat. I sat and we both stared at each other for what seemed like an eternity. Eventually he said, "Gwen, I don't know what to say. I don't know how it happened, but you are going to have a baby." Before the words could even finish rolling out of his mouth I jumped straight up! I remember my exact words as though it were yesterday, "Do I laugh or cry?" He responded, "Laugh if you are happy and cry if you don't want the baby." Instantly I began to laugh and cry because it was the happiest day of my life. From that day forward nothing has made me happier than hearing the news I so desperately had been waiting to hear, that I was going to be a mama.

I was still laughing and crying when I left the doctor's office as I passed several people walking to my car. Some stopped to ask if they could help while others just stopped and looked. Although I saw them, because I was so elated, it was if they were all transparent. I felt alive, inspired, and so loved. I think I sped all the way home and couldn't get in the house fast enough. All I could think about was calling my family and spreading the good news. My first call was made to my husband. Twenty four years ago cell phones were not as plentiful as they are now so I had to page my husband because he was at one of the local high schools giving physical exams. Just as I knew he would, he called me back immediately. When I answered the phone he heard my voice and knew. After speaking with my husband and hearing the excitement in his voice I became even more eager so I began the many phone calls to my parents and my sisters. And as expected, everyone was excited for us.

I was thirty-five years old when Dalen was born. I had a wonderful pregnancy for a woman my age giving birth to her first child. My bundle of joy made his entrance at 3:05 a.m. on Monday, March 18, 1985 at 7lbs., 14 oz., 21 inches long, with a head full of curly black hair. Even though my sister Katie said even monkeys think their babies are cute, I knew with everything in me that Dalen was beautiful. When Dalen came into my life, I had already done many of the things in life that I wanted to do. I had gotten my "run" out. I wanted to be a mother; I wanted to be the best mother a baby could have. I loved Dalen more than life itself. He needed me and I needed and wanted him.

For the first three to four weeks, my husband was very attentive to the baby and me. I felt as if I were on top of the world. I felt life didn't owe me anything but I had everything I wanted and needed. Slowly, my husband's time at home started to decrease again. He started coming home later and later from work, while some nights he wouldn't even come home at all. I was so busy with Dalen and trying to be a good mother that it took me some time to zero in on my husband's behavior. The nights he didn't come home, he didn't report to work the next day either. His secretaries would call and ask for him, telling me that the office was full with patients. I would have to tell the office staff that he didn't come home the night before and that I hadn't talked with him, so I had no idea where he was. This same behavior went on for several months. I couldn't share it with my family because I was too ashamed, but I knew there was definitely a problem, I just had no idea what it was. And just like anyone else without any further rational would, I began to suspect it was another woman.

Me being the strong woman I had always proclaimed to be, I just sucked up my emotions and closed off my thoughts and promised to myself no matter what, with or without my husband, I was going to be the best mother I could possibly be. Dalen was a blessing from God that I so desperately wanted, and there was nothing and no one that could tear apart our bond. Time slowly went on and I watched as the days turned into months and the months into years, as my husbands behavior and habits consistently went downhill. My greatest fear as the years passed us by, and Dalen grew older, was that one day my son would look to me for answers in regards to his father absence, and I would have no response. All I could do was pray that when that day came, id be ready.

Part 2 – Dalen
Earliest Memories of My Father

Even at a young age I knew my household was designed differently from those of my friends. It was myself, my mother and father, and my grandmother all living together under one roof. I guess one could assume that it was an "extended family household," except for the fact that my father would only be home a few days out of the week. It was almost as if this home that my mother tried so hard to hold together was just an extended-stay motel to this man.

At first, I didn't realize that my family was any different than the next, until I started spending time with my friends and their families. Throughout my elementary childhood I had three solid friends whom I spent time with outside of school, and they all had different family setups. I had one friend whose mother had passed away when he was a baby and he was left to live with his father and twin sister. I had a second friend who was white, who lived with his mother, father, and little brother. Then I had a third friend who was an only child like myself but lived with his mother and father only. I was able to pick up on small things that each of these families had that my household was lacking. It is truly amazing what a child can subconsciously pick up on at such an early age. I saw in my first friend the yearning and need for a strong woman figure in his life. Every chance he got he was trying to come over to my house and be around myself, my mother, and my grandmother. He hated being around his father. I really don't know why he didn't like his father; he never really spoke about it. I just think his father didn't show him any compassion or attention. Every time I would go to his house his father would never interact with my friend or his sister. It was almost as if they were raising themselves. Although I didn't know what a Blessing was back then, I did know that I had something special that some people would kill for - a loving mother.

Within my second friends' family, my white friend, I saw what I thought a family really was supposed to be. I mean it was just like the movies. He had a mother and father who were always home. He had a younger brother and a little sister on the way. His family even had a golden retriever! In my mind families like that only existed on the television screens. Even the Huxtables didn't have a golden retriever. Every time I spent time at his house the whole family would do activities. We would always play games and watch movies and do all sorts of fun things as a group. I remember thinking to myself way back then that when I had a family, I was going to make sure we always came together and had a good time.

Then there was my third friend. This friend outlasted the other two throughout my elementary school growth and development. The thing about this friend that connected us both was the fact that we were both only children. By having this in common we could really relate to one another. The difference between me and him was that every time I went to his house his father was always there. Any school activity we had, his father was there. Any sporting event we went to, his father was there. Now by no means am I saying that his family had no problems and everything was perfect, I am just speaking on my interpretation of the situation as a seven or eight year old.

With me being at such a young age I was naïve to a lot of things. For instance, I knew my father was only home a few days out of the week but I just figured he was either at work or doing something work related. It wasn't until one summer day that one of my friends shed light onto my family situation and rained on my parade. It was my friend whose mother had passed away that really opened my eyes. I remember it like it was yesterday. We were in the garage playing with a magnifying glass and burning ants and trying to light incense sticks while my mother and grandmother were in the house. Right in the middle of me trying to burn a hole in his shoe with the magnifying glass he looked up at me and asked, "So Dalen, where does your dad be at all the time?" That question kind of caught me off guard. I never really thought about where he could be, I just figured he was working. I gave him the only response I could think of, "I guess at work." My friend then began to ask me questions like, "Is he ever home?" "Why is he never here?" At this point I couldn't answer any more of his questions. It wasn't like I was becoming emotional or anything; I just didn't know any of the answers. I just told him, "I don't know, he's usually here two or three days out of the week." With this response a huge bomb was dropped by my friend. "Man, Dalen, your dad has another family!" He then stated with a huge grin on his face, "I mean think about it, he's never around! Where else is he sleeping every night?" I didn't know what to think. That was something I would have never fathomed by myself. It surely did open my eyes to the situation and made me realize that maybe something wasn't right. I never told my mother about that conversation. I just always kept it to myself locked in the back of my mind. Thinking back on the situation now, that was a conversation that was not needed to be discussed by two eight or nine year olds. Honestly, that conversation just proved to me that my friend was way more advanced and more cognitive about his surroundings than myself.

After the conversation with my friend I convinced myself that I was going to start paying way more attention to the happenings around me. Over the next weeks, months, and years I began to outline my fathers' habits and schedule in my mind. By the time the sixth and seventh grade rolled around I could almost predict when my father would walk through the door, how long he would stay, and when he would be leaving back out again. I had it down to an exact science. It was almost religious. Life was great when he wasn't around. It would be me, my mother, and my grandmother. We enjoyed one another. The house would be filled with laughter and conversation. What was considered a utopia would quickly turn into a war zone whenever my father would return home. He would enter the house reeking of past days' worth of unexcused debauchery. He would stroll into our home, his extended-stay motel, at the wee hours of the morning sneaking past my room and barging into the master suite that housed my sleeping mother. From the confines of my bed I would hear arguing. I would hear my mother telling her husband sternly to "get out!" or to "leave me alone!" After what would seem like an eternity of them going back and forth, it would never fail; their door would swing open, and out would come this man. I would immediately shut my eyes and play sleep when I heard him walking through the halls. And like clockwork he would come to the breezeway of my room and call out to me to see if I was sleep. Once I made it known that he had awakened me, he would come into my room reeking of alcohol and politely whisper to me "Son, do you have any money I can borrow?" At that age I didn't have a job, so all the money I did have would be from doing small chores and keeping the change when my mother went to the grocery store. To me, my life savings of $30 was my only and everything. It was the only sense of true value I had at that time. It is funny that I possessed the same qualities at such an early age that I hold dear to my heart still this day. To this day I am the type of person that will give you my last, all the way to the shirt off my back. I guess that can be a blessing and a curse. Some people quickly forget the true act of kindness that you show. I would ease my way out the bed and ask my father to please step out of the room so I could go to my secret hiding place to retrieve the money. He would humor my wishes and politely step outside the room closing the door behind him. I would then open the door to my closet and reach high onto the top shelf and pull out the case that once held the first and only musical instrument I ever played, the recorder I took home from music class. After emptying my makeshift piggy bank I would open the door and hand my father the money. It was almost as if I was a kiddy loan shark, minus the team of leg breaking enforcers to send out when my money wasn't returned.

Beyond the memory of my first business as a child being the sole proprietor of the BOD (Bank of Dalen), I remember questioning the simple awareness of my father, asking myself if he even knew his own son's birthday. It seemed to me that if my mother had not handed me my birthday card, with both signatures being somewhat mockingly obviously scribbled in the same handwriting, in front of him, he may not have known my birthday from any other random Tuesday. It was a time in my life when I did not think my father even knew my name. I know my last statement may seem as if I am taking my feelings too far, but I can only write what I honestly thought growing up. From as long as I could remember all the way through high school my father referred to me as "Boy." For some reason this title mentally scarred me. Even at a young age I knew something was not right about that word. Although I was a child, and essentially a little "boy" at the time, the connotation I felt he was using the word in made me feel worthless and beneath him. It was not until I entered junior high school that I started doing my research and found out that the term "boy" was a form of verbal abuse that had its origins in the slave era. White slave owners would call any black man, no matter what age, boy to imply that they were not men. These slave owners felt that these people were a piece of property and not worthy enough to be called a man. Not to compare my father to a slave owner but I felt that his usage of the word was meant to mentally suppress me. I remember being in my room and hearing him yell, "Boy, get in here," or him standing right in front of me stuttering over my name and using "boy" as a simple alternative. It was almost as if my father tried everything in his power to push me away from him. It seemed to me that he would go out of his way to demoralize and antagonize me. Knowing that I was an only child and had no friends in my immediate area, my father would go out of his way to tell me to get out of "grown folks" business or go find someone my own age, whenever I just sincerely wanted to be around my parents.

Those statements quickly set the precedent for our relationship. Even as a child, I could take a hint. To me it seemed as if I was just genuinely not wanted. For the life of me I could never really figure out why my father's other two children would never come around. It wasn't until I reached my high school years that my question was quickly answered. I finally came to understand that the man that brought me into this world, just genuinely did not know how to be a father. He came from a long line of men who were not stand up guys when it came to their families, so I guess I really couldn't fault him. He was merely a product of his upbringing. When a child is not given the love and affection and support he so desperately yearns for, only two things can happen when he/she reaches adulthood. Either that adult will fall into the same pattern that he/she grew up seeing or they will learn from the mistakes of their elders and break the vicious cycle. I was determined to end that family curse.

Part 3 – Preschool to Elementary

Gwen

I can't remember the exact day my uninvited and unexpected houseguest arrived to announce its plans to live with us for what seemed a lifetime. That guest formally introduced herself to me as cocaine. I didn't have a working knowledge of drugs because I had always been careful to keep away from people known to use them of any kind. Unfortunately, my husband and I are as different as night and day, but as weird as it may sound, we always complimented each other. He told me later that a woman had introduced him to drugs.

By the time I felt the need to investigate my husband's decrease in time spent at home, it was too late. Cocaine, my uninvited and unexpected houseguest, had moved in and set up residence with my husband. He allowed this family destroyer, this relationship slayer, this kidnapper of a father to invade our home environment. Luckily, my husband never did drugs in our home or in Dalen's presence. I think I would literally have killed him if he had. I would have done whatever I had to in order to protect Dalen from this uninvited and unwelcomed houseguest.

Days turned into weeks, weeks became months and months became years. Dalen and I began to see my husband, his father, less and less. Dalen would stand at the window watching and asking for his father. The constant abandonment caused me and my son to become extremely lonely. During this time of loneliness, I became so filled with anger and bitterness that I made a difficult decision. I decided Dalen would not suffer simply because his father had a love and need for cocaine more than he had for his family. I set in my mind to always be there for my son, stepping into both parental roles.

My mind carried me back to memories of my childhood, where my father was gone a lot from us. My mother served as both parents to her nine daughters, and as a result none of us were ever hooked on drugs and we never went to jail. We all turned out okay. I told myself that if my mother could do it, so could I. Therefore, I undertook the job of rearing Dalen all by myself.

My first duty was to make Dalen feel loved; something we all have a need for. God created us out of love. When there is a lack of love, there is a void. If that void is not filled, we as humans go looking for something that gives us satisfaction to fill it. I didn't want Dalen to look for satisfaction; I just wanted him to know how much both his parents loved him.

As time progressed I made another decision. I decided never to talk bad about my husband in Dalen's presence. In order for Dalen to grow into manhood, I knew I had to give him the time and attention he needed. I was always sure to hug and kiss Dalen several times each day, while constantly telling him how much I loved him. To that end, when I had to leave him, I only left him with family members I knew loved him and would reinforce my love. The word of God says, "Love bears all things, believes all things, hopes all things, endures all things; love never fails" (1st Corinthians 13:7-8). A son who feels loved is the first step into manhood.

I strongly believe that in every boy lays a spirit of adventure. Dalen was not the exception to the rule. He loved to try new and exciting things. I grew to be very concerned about him because he seemed to lack fear in all areas. The elementary school Dalen attended had a Boy Scout Troop and of course, he wanted very much to be a part of it. Dalen, being the type of person that doesn't accept no easily, finally wore me down. I gave in and allowed him to become a Boy Scout. It wasn't that I didn't *want* him to be one; I knew the boys would be engaging in some activities that only their fathers could be part of. I didn't want Dalen to be disappointed when his father couldn't be found. No mother wants to see her child repeatedly disappointed or sitting on the sideline wanting desperately to be a part. Mothers can do a lot of things that fathers can, yet there are some things only a father can do.

This story cannot be told unless I digress for a short time to tell you a little more about myself. God plays a major role in my life. Shortly after my husband's drug problem became unbearable for me, I knew I needed help to make it through what I thought would be a very short period of time. Boy was I wrong. I began searching for the help, the peace and guidance, that I needed. I needed a husband and Dalen needed a father. Some of my family members and closest friends suggested I divorce my husband, take myself from him and get as far as I could from him. I contemplated the idea of divorce, but I couldn't bring myself to file for one.

I kept being reminded of my first divorce and how hard it was for me. Even though my first husband had been very abusive, I thank God I was able to get out of the marriage with my life and a sound, healthy mind. Besides, the idea of being be a young black woman, twice divorced and in her early thirties with a young child seemed absurd to me.

Although my husband had a drug addiction, I knew he loved Dalen and me unconditionally; no one could tell me differently. Because of my love for Dalen, I felt no other man would allow me to do the things for him that I wanted to do. No other man would allow me to spend the time with Dalen I had become accustomed to. I knew Dalen needed time to grow and develop without feeling like he wasn't a part of my life or our family. I couldn't split my time between Dalen and a third husband, so I made the decision to stay married to Dalen's father. It was a marriage in name only because I was living a single life. I resigned myself to this way of living. I was too busy with Dalen and work to be focused on being lonely. Still, I needed wisdom and guidance.

My elderly mother lived with us for fifteen years which, of course, was a blessing for me. She provided more love for Dalen and was a source of wisdom and strength for me as a married woman living single. As a result, Dalen never came home to an empty house; there as always a mature adult home who loved him.

Dalen

American journalist Sydney J. Harris once stated, "The commonest fallacy among women is that simply having children makes them a mother - which is as absurd as believing that having a piano makes one a musician." I truly believe with everything in my heart that some women are born mothers. Some women are just born with that loving and nurturing instinct that is needed to be a great mother. I can honestly say that I am extremely blessed to have been born to such a great woman who exudes all the qualities needed to be considered not only a great mother, but as a best friend as well.

When I begin to think of my mother, words from Washington Irving immediately come to mind; "A mother is the truest friend we have, when trials, heavy and sudden, fall upon us; when adversity takes the place of prosperity; when friends who rejoice with us in our sunshine, desert us when troubles thicken around us, still will she cling to us, and endeavor by her kind precepts and counsels to dissipate the clouds of darkness, and cause peace to return to our hearts." My mother instilled in me at an early age that she would always be there for me through thick and thin. She made it known that whether I was wrong or right she would always stick by my side, and for that I am grateful. Starting at an early age my mother established a relationship with me built around trust and love. She made sure that the lines of communication were always open no matter what the topic may have been. I found myself telling her things about my life and daily routine that one would only tell their best friend. It truly amazed me that my mother never judged me. It was almost as if as long as I told her what I had done in advance I was not punished. It seemed like I almost started telling on myself. That was just the type of relationship I had with my mother. I trusted her.

Just like most sons, I loved my mother with all my heart. Although I considered her my best friend, she was also a huge disciplinarian. With her being my only parent that was consistently around she had to set some type of parental boundaries, and she was notorious for not sparing the rod. I knew my mother loved me to death and would do any and everything for me, but I knew once I really messed up, the other side of her would come out. What was once a sweet woman who I could tell any and everything to would almost instantly turn into a Bible-toting belt-slinging mother who demanded her respect and would settle for nothing less than a well-mannered son. With my mother playing both the role of friend and parent, I could do nothing but respect her. It got to the point in my life when I hated to disappoint my mother. The thought of me letting her down brought more pain to me than a beating ever could, and she knew it.

As the years passed by, and my father became more and more absent, my relationship with my mother continued to grow stronger and more solid. We both knew the turmoil in our home and could sincerely relate to one another. We understood each other, and we always knew that through thick and thin that we would be there for one another. We were a team. We were each other's support system. This was all during a time in both of our lives when we began to embark on new beginnings. I was starting to get more involved and dedicated to sports while my mother was focusing on getting her church off the ground and spreading God's word. Just as much as my mother was in the stands cheering me on, I was just as equally in the crowd every Sunday showing my support of her dream and new career path.

> *"The relationship of a son towards both of his parents is very complex. A son will likely feel a close bond with his mother, yet see his father as an adversary and competitor.*

When a son sees how his father interacts with his mother he will either attempt to model his father's behavior or reject his father's example of relationships with women. From the parents' point of view, having a son can be one of the greatest joys they will ever experience, but also one of the greatest challenges. Balancing the need to offer freedom to your son while placing appropriate boundaries may be an area of contention."

- FamilyFriendPoems.com

Although my mother was raised eighth of nine girls, and was not reared around any young men, she was still able to effectively relate to me and guide me as a young boy growing into a grown man. Growing up around all women, my mother was able to witness the different types of men that would come in and out of her sisters' lives. She was able to discern the qualities of a gentleman and the traits of a dog. These templates along with the corruption and deterioration of her first marriage taught my mother the characteristics and manners that a true gentleman holds dear to his heart. My mother was able to successfully instill in me bits and pieces of wisdom and truth daily, by just reliving her past experiences. It was as if all the bad she had seen allowed for her to realize all the potential for good that a decent young man could possess. Coupling her past experiences with a strong relationship with her Heavenly Father, my mother was determined to raise me into the man that God had intended for me to be.

Gwen

Trouble will do one of two things for you: it will bring you closer to Jesus or it will take you completely away from him. I allowed my trouble to bring me closer to Jesus. I wanted more than just attending church on Sundays. I wanted to personally know this man that I had read about and had heard ministers preach about. So I set out on a mission to meet the man, Jesus. I began to attend a home Bible Study with a few ladies and little by little, I was introduced to Jesus. After being introduced, I knew I wanted and needed a personal relationship with Him.

I used every spare minute I had to read and study God's word. After reading and studying God's word, I knew I had found the missing piece of the puzzle. Jesus provided the guidance, direction, wisdom and peace I so desperately yearned for. He was everything I needed and more. Dalen needed a father and I needed a husband, so I asked Jesus to be my husband and Dalen's daddy. With this new found revelation, I began to pray about everything that concerned Dalen and me.

Now back to boy scouting. Boy scouting had become very important to Dalen, as with the other seven year olds in his troop, it was a big part of his life. He received several badges and wore them proudly on his little navy blue shirt. After months of training and survival exercises, Dalen's troop leader decided it was time for the boys to have a father/son camping trip. As I stated earlier, there are some things a mother cannot do; there must be a father or a good father image, this was one of those instances. Dalen's heart was dead set on being a part of this father/son camping trip. The only problem we faced was no father. I couldn't allow myself to think that Dalen wouldn't be a part of something so exciting and grand for a little boy. I knew I couldn't sign him up because his father was incapable of showing up. This would be too devastating, so I did what I knew to do, I prayed and explained to God how disappointed Dalen would be if he had to miss the camping trip. Remember, I had asked Jesus to be Dalen's father and my husband. It was His responsibility to make a way for Dalen to go, and I trusted him.

Mothers, when you find yourself rearing a young boy all by yourself, it is very important that you have Godly young men and women, who can be trusted, to surround you and your family. When needing help with your young son, identify someone in the church or someone close to you, get to know them and do a background check if necessary. I happened to know the perfect young man to ask for help, a gentleman I had taught in Bible Study. He had a quiet and gentle spirit and he had several brothers and sisters of his own. After much prayer and meditation, I knew this young man was the one to accompany Dalen on his Boy Scout camping trip.

Once the decision was made, I set out to purchase everything Dalen and this young man would need for their big event. I went to one of the largest sporting goods chains in the Dallas area, and wandered aimlessly down the aisle trying to figure out what one would need to go camping. Since I had never gone camping before, I was totally clueless. I was blessed to have a sales person who understood my situation and patiently assisted me in getting the needed items.

At last the big day arrived. Dalen and the young man accompanied the other scouts and their fathers to the camping site. The young man was given all the help he needed from the other fathers to set up the tent and prepare the other things. I didn't worry about Dalen though I did send up a prayer. Dalen had a wonderful time; he got the chance to do everything the other scouts did with their fathers. Let him tell it, he didn't even miss not having his own father there.

Most children will accept a substitute if they know they will be allowed to do the things they desire to do and spend time with their friends. The key is the mother spending time with the substitute, getting to know him and developing a relationship with him for the sake of her child.

Dalen

It's funny how the mind works. Some people can remember experiences as far back as the age of two or three. As for myself, I have a few memories from the ages of four and five but for the most part my memory kicks in around the beginning of elementary school. At this point in my life I was enrolled in a predominantly White private school.

In the first grade I can honestly say I was, for a lack of a better term, "color blind" when it came to realizing I was one of the few Black kids running around the playground. I just wanted to have fun and do whatever it was the other kids were doing at that time. The school I attended did not have any sports for children in grades first through third, but their positive alternative was the Boy Scouts of America. Thinking back on it now, I don't even think I realized what that organization really stood for. I all I knew was that all my friends, who were predominantly White, and one Black friend-- my best friend at that time was going to join. There was no way I was going to let everyone be a part of something that seemed to be so much fun without me.

After being introduced to this organization that promised to "Build Tomorrow's Leaders," I rushed home and told my mother all about it. To my dismay it seemed that all of my excitement and enthusiasm was drowned out by her solemn, "oh ok's" and "we'll see's." I couldn't for the life of me understand why I couldn't just get a simple YES out of her. I mean, it was the Boy Scouts for goodness sake, who wouldn't allow their child to be a part of something so cool, something so great, something so American! I was determined to be one of tomorrow's leaders. With the registration deadline rapidly approaching I kept pestering my mother. Finally she gave in. I was officially going to be a Cub Scout!

To me, the Boy Scouts was just another activity that allowed me as an only child to spend time with some of my friends outside of the school yard. We were able to do a lot of activities and learn a lot of interesting things. After weeks and weeks of activities, I started to notice small things. I would notice how when the other fathers would drop their sons off at the meetings they would come inside and check our progress and speak with our troop leader. Me on the other hand, I didn't even think my father knew I was a part of the Cub Scouts. We never discussed it. All I knew was that when it came time to go to the meetings my mother was there to drop me off and pick me up. She was never late, she never missed a beat.

After months and months of training and meetings, my troop leader thought it was time for us to put our survival techniques into practice. It was time for the Father-Son camping trip. I was excited! This was the first time I had ever been camping. The troop leader was telling us all of the things we were going to be doing. The activities ranged from father-son three legged races to father-son fishing competition, to father-son tent building exercises. All of this seemed perfect to me except for the fact that this man kept throwing out the terminology "father-son." Then reality set in. I wasn't sure if I was going to able to make this trip. I didn't even know where my father was most of the time. So I did what any child would do in that situation. I asked a question. "So what if my father is working that weekend? Could my mother come?" I mean I may have been young back then but I wasn't dumb. I knew not to tell these random people my family business, so I just hypothetically blamed it on work; like I always had before. Unfortunately my troop leader explained to me that it was only for men and that girls wouldn't want to be outside doing all those type of things. I politely smiled and nodded. I knew with everything in me that the mother I had would have been the first person at that camp site fumbling through instructions on how to build a tent if she could.

When I got home that evening and gave my mother the information on the trip and asked her about me going, she politely replied "Yes Dalen, you are going. I promise you that." Unlike my father, if my mother made a promise to me it was as good as gold. The big day finally arrived and just like I had expected, I hadn't seen my father in two whole days. I began to become very upset and disappointed. I was more upset at myself for even allowing myself to get my hopes up. I felt like everyone had let me down, my father for not showing up, myself for getting my hopes up, and my mother for breaking a promise. Little did I know my mother already had it worked out. When it was time for me to leave to go on the trip there was a knock at the door. When my mother answered the door there was this young guy who I would always see at

Bible study. My mother informed me that he would be taking me on the trip. I really didn't know the guy like my mother did but at that age I was just happy to be going, I didn't care who took me. We arrived at the camp ground and hit the road running. We participated in all events and even won a few! It wasn't until a question was asked to me by one of the other scouts that I was drug right back to reality. "Dalen, who is that guy you are with? He's too young to be your dad." The question caught me off guard and for the life of me I could not remember his name. Me being the child I was I responded with, "I don't know, he goes to my church," and that was the end of that conversation. No one brought it up anymore. Thinking back on it now, I know the kids probably went back and told their dads and the troop leader but no one ever brought it up again. I respect them for that. I respect them for understanding that not everyone comes from a perfect situation and not making a huge deal about who brought me. They just let me be a kid and have fun with my friends, and for that, to this day I am grateful.

Part 4 – Junior High

Gwen

Just like with any other child, Dalen's attention and interest quickly shifted to the next exciting thing, sports. Basketball is the preferred game of most boys. Dalen went from being a boy scout to wanting to be the next Michael Jordan. He started playing basketball in the third grade. All of his friends played, so naturally he didn't want to be left on the sideline. Of all the activities he participated in, I honestly believe basketball meant more to him than anything else. With an absent father, I had the job of taking Dalen to practice. I never missed a practice session or any of his games. My sister and niece went as well; still there was something missing. Dalen always tried to spot his father by my side whenever I entered the gymnasium. Truth be told, my husband only attended a handful of Dalen's games.

I didn't allow my husband's absence to overshadow Dalen or steal his joy. I enrolled Dalen in very basketball camp I could find. My sister and I even took the time to take him to Washington, D.C. for an entire week so he could attend the camp at Georgetown, his dream college. We stayed in a hotel close to the school because Dalen had never been away from home without me, his grandparents or his aunts. By no means was Dalen a junior Michael Jordan, but I wanted him to feel good about himself so I went the extra mile. Mothers should always try with everything in them to make their children feel good about their endeavors, however big or small.

You don't have to be a Michael Jordan to feel good about yourself in basketball. The parent's role is to encourage, support and love, no matter what. I encouraged Dalen to try whatever interested him. Once he made the decision to try, I supported him. I encouraged Dalen by talking with him and making his interest my own. I wanted him to understand no one would ever be great in all things, so he should do his absolute best and have fun doing it. So Dalen had a lot of fun playing basketball and football. He knew he would not disappoint me, so he was free to just be a child and fully enjoy himself. My love for Dalen wasn't going to change just because he was unable to make fifteen or twenty points in a game. Our children should not disappoint us if they are not highly skilled in areas we as parents, would like them to be. We should love, encourage and support them always. I never forced Dalen to participate in anything he wasn't comfortable doing or wanted to do other than something educational that would benefit him later in life. Children seem to mature faster when they are able to make some of their own decisions. My love for Dalen always made him feel as though he was equal to everyone, as smart as anyone else and able to do what anyone else could do.

I can honestly say Dalen and I talked a lot. Unlike some parents, I talked *with* him, not at him. Talking with someone allows for two-way communication; each person responding to the other, both people being allowed to contribute to the conversation. Talking *at* someone is a one-person conversation with a few poorly injected yeses or nos. Effortlessly asking your child a question that invokes a simple "yes" or "no" answer is not communication.

I couldn't wait to pick Dalen up from school because I wanted to know everything that happened during the school day. I wanted to know what he had for lunch, who he played with at recess, or if anyone had hurt his feelings that day. I wanted to create an atmosphere in which Dalen felt free to talk with me about anything. Dalen is now twenty-four years old and still feels free to ask me questions and tell me anything. So much so that even at the age of fifty-eight, I still blush. Children have a voice; they want to be heard; they must be heard. As parents, if we don't allow our children to talk with us or spend time with us, they will find someone else to talk with and share their time with. In most cases, the person they find is not the one we would choose for our children. Sometimes that person may lead our child down the wrong path. I have always been of the opinion that children are miniature adults, they need the same things we need, they experience the same emotions and feelings we do only on a smaller level. Children hurt; cry, love, get angry, and sometimes they just genuinely don't want to be bothered.

For as long as I can remember, Dalen has been a child who has held grudges. My biggest battle with him has been trying to help him, or should I say trying to convince him, to let go of all the anger and unforgiveness he allowed to build up in his heart because of his father's absence in his life and in our home. When Dalen was growing up, he would stand at the window and watch for his father to come home; but most nights, his efforts were done in vain, because his father never came. When he did come home, Dalen would be extremely happy. I can remember his face lighting up when he told his father about upcoming games or activities. He never failed to ask his father if he would attend. His father always gave the same answer, "Yes, I will be there." I knew with everything in me he had the intention to be there, but the uninvited and unexpected houseguest had other plans for him that would not allow him to pull himself away.

Remember, children are miniature adults and can only handle so many rejections and disappointments before they develop some kind of defense mechanism to protect themselves. Dalen allowed anger to become his defense. As an older child, he became so angry with his father that he didn't want to talk with him during those times that they were home together. Usually, Dalen didn't even want to be home when his father was there. This was the hardest part of my life; living with someone who has a drug problem and watching my son use anger and sometimes hate as a defense. Because of my close walk with Jesus, I knew what anger and hate could eventually do to my son. I didn't want

Dalen going through adolescence and adulthood full of hate and anger. I knew if this was prolonged in Dalen's life, he could have the potential to be a danger to himself and anyone around him. Because anger is such a dangerous enemy, I had to help Dalen overcome this thing that had gripped him by force and without his permission, and was causing him to behave in ways that were not true to his character.

I set out on a mission of rescue. Dalen needed help; he couldn't help himself and was too entangled in the web to understand how deadly this could be for him. I knew from reading God's word and working with His people that love covers a multitude of sins. I also knew that love bears all things, believes all things, hopes all things, endures all things, and that love never fails. My mission was to try and help Dalen understand that his father really loved and cared for him and that his absence had nothing to do with Dalen. I made a conscious effort to never say anything negative about his father in front of him. I never came against my husband when he was home and disciplined Dalen. My mission was also to show Dalen his father and me were in total agreement when it came to him. I wanted Dalen to see I trusted my husband's love for him and that he could trust that love as well.

I must admit this mission was not completed in one day, one week, one month or even one year. It took years for God to deliver Dalen of all the anger and unforgiveness. Today, Dalen is a very strong, loving, healthy twenty-four year old with a very bright future ahead of him. I believe Dalen will be a great father someday and I look forward to being an excellent grandmother to his children. I know with everything in me Dalen will also be a great husband. There are many good things his father taught him indirectly about being a man and a husband and the things he should do for his wife and family. Dalen was and still is a fast learner, and I know he will spoil his children as I did him, but in a good way. Dalen till this day tells me how grateful he is for the activities he participated in and the hardships he encountered growing up, for without them he doesn't feel like he would be the well rounded individual he is today.

Dalen

After a few more months of Cub Scouts I did what most other young boys would do; I moved on to the next interesting activity. That activity was basketball. Over the next seven years basketball played an instrumental part in my life. Like most boys my age, I had it all figured out. I was going to play basketball all the way through elementary, carry it on into Jr. High, then become a powerhouse in high school. After high school, Georgetown University was supposed to beat down my door and beg me to accept their athletic scholarship. After two years at Georgetown University Coach John Thompson was supposed to sit me down and discuss my next step into the NBA. Yeah, I had it all figured out - least that's what I thought.

Basketball over the next few years seemed to be very reminiscent of my Cub Scout days. I fell into the same almost exact routine. My mother would take me to practice and be there when we let out. She came to all games no matter where they were located. I could always count on looking up in the bleachers and seeing her smiling back at me. Now don't get me wrong, my father did show up to a few basketball games. I will give credit where credit is due. When it came to sports I did have the support of a few of my other family members. My mothers' sister and her daughter would come to just about all my games. It was always good to know that I did have some kind of support system in the stands. After a short while I started to become a tad bit envious of my teammates. I would see all the fathers in the stands cheering for their sons and telling them to bend their knees while at the free throw line. At halftime the other fathers would come out of the bleachers to give their sons simple words of encouragement. I tried to not let it bother me. I just would look up to my fan club in the stands and one smile or head nod of approval from my mother and I was back focused again. She was always there.

As the seasons changed and the years passed by, I became more passionate about basketball. I would practice every day and play pickup games every chance I could. I was actually a pretty decent and dedicated player. While attending private school, I was always considered one of the best on the team. I would try and attend every basketball camp and clinic that my mother would allow me to sign up for. It wasn't until the summer of my eight grade year that my eyes were truly opened. Up until this point in my life I hadn't had any real competition. I was used to playing basketball in a small private school league. I was totally oblivious to the outside world and the athletes that inhabited that space. Some kind of way I got wind that my dream college Georgetown University was hosting a summer basketball camp in Washington D.C. I had to go. This was my chance to impress the coaches there. I spoke with my mother about it, and to my surprise she was all for it. One thing about my mother, she has always supported me in any and everything I have been a part of. She had never made me feel inadequate in any shape, form, or fashion. If I wanted to do something or achieve some type of aspiration she would go out of her way to show support and help me reach my dreams. I truly believe that if I wanted to walk on the moon she would have built me a spaceship. After a few short months of waiting, our departure date had arrived. My mother, my aunt, and I boarded an airplane and headed to D.C.

My arrival at Georgetown University quickly turned into a jaw dropping, culture shocking, and life altering revelation. I was quickly launched into an intense program with other kids who were supposedly my age. You couldn't pay me to believe that these giants, these aliens, these 14 year old 6'5" MEN, were actually my competition. You could have never paid me to believe that there were actually kids my age that tall. It was at that exact moment that reality set in and I started to question my abilities. Now please do not misinterpret my words or misunderstand what I am saying. I do believe that you should always have faith in what you are doing and try your best to succeed, but in my case that day, I knew my dream was over. I think at that moment I understood what a realist actually was. Although growing up my mother always instilled in me that quitters never prospered, I just knew deep inside that God had greater plans for me.

Gwen

Junior High was the darkest time for Dalen and me. After returning from the basketball camp at Georgetown University, it seemed as if Dalen's whole attitude toward the sport had changed. What was once an extreme passion and driving force in his life merely turned into a hobby simply done for recreation. It was blatantly obvious that Dalen was no longer a little boy, but had developed into a teenager. He became friends with teen-aged boys who had various personalities. I had to make some adjustments in my life and change my way of thinking as it pertained to Dalen. Yes, sometimes we as parents have to change our way of doing things to keep up with the life-changing experiences our teenagers transcend through. I had to allow Dalen to choose his own friends even though there was one in particular I had concerns about. But life taught me a long time ago the more you try to separate two people, the more they will find a way to be together. Parents, unless the bond between you and your child is made of steel, a hole can be made in it. Remember, there are times when even the steel can be dented.

Dalen had always attended private school. Private school worked well for Dalen until the first six weeks of his 8th grade year. My husband and I made the decision, after careful thought, to transfer Dalen to public school. This decision lent itself to much conversation with my family and friends resulting in a 50/50 split. Nevertheless, the decision was made. Dalen was quietly withdrawn from private school and registered at his new school. The one good thing that came out of the transfer was Dalen would be able to do something he had always wanted to do: ride a big yellow school bus with the other neighborhood children.

Dalen made the adjustment rather fast. He made new friends, which now meant two sets of friends for both of us to contend with. Let me explain; I knew Dalen's friends from private school, the ones I felt good about and the ones who gave me a burden in my spirit where my son was concerned. Now I had to get to know the new friends to determine which ones I got a check in my spirit about. Parents, always try to learn as much as possible about your children's friends as they will have more of an impact than you or any other adult in their lives.

I knew how Dalen felt about his father, so I couldn't afford to alienate Dalen from me. I couldn't allow him to think I didn't love him or trust him. One of the teenage boys that Dalen befriended caused my spirit a double check. My husband had always been able to "read" people and was excellent at judging character. When he met Dalen's friend, he had the same concerns in his spirit. I didn't tell Dalen because I didn't want to add fuel to a fire that was burning on its own. Besides, Dalen thought his friend was the best thing since sliced bread.

This young man was allowed to do what he wanted when he wanted. Money was no issue for this young man. He walked daily with more money in his pocket than most grown men. This was exciting to Dalen. I knew from all this that as a mother, I had to intercede for Dalen but without his knowledge. So I started doing what I do best then and what I do best now... I began to pray. I asked God to separate Dalen and the young man. The separation didn't happen overnight, so I prayed continuously. A parent's prayer will work when nothing else will. God says we have not because we ask not.

Dalen could have gone over fool's hill during his Junior High years if God had not given me the wisdom to deal with him and his friends. As I dealt with protecting Dalen, I also began to deal with my feelings of anger and resentment towards my husband. I began to blame him for everything that was going wrong in our family. I felt his drug addiction had done this to what I had always dreamed would be the "perfect family." I have learned in my later years there is no such thing as a perfect family, a perfect child, or a perfect spouse. All we have is love and forgiveness.

It's funny how things work sometimes. What started off as me attending church services and Bible studies religiously, seamlessly led to me having the want and desire to spread my knowledge and understandings. With one person willing to listen and learn, I began my very own weekly Bible study. As the weeks went by, more and more people added to the congregation. What was once a class of one sitting at my dining room table, quickly transitioned into dozens and dozens of people making my living room and kitchen standing room only.

I was perfectly happy being a one night a week Bible-study teacher in my home every Friday night when I began to serve a greater call on my life. Even though I felt this greater call on my life, and the people in the fifty-member Bible study class began to call me pastor, I tried to run from it. I didn't want any more responsibility in my life. I was already married to a drug addict and parenting a son all alone, I just felt that I couldn't handle anything else. Another reason I didn't want to accept the call of a full time pastor was because I was very happy in my present career. I was a third grade teacher, with the hope of becoming an elementary school principal.

After a couple months of no peace and rest, I finally gave in to the burden that I couldn't shake loose of. I sincerely said yes God to your will, I will do whatever you want me to do.

Being a woman Pastor is almost as hard as being a mother raising a child all alone. I compare the two because both are lonely jobs. Jobs that some men feel women are unable to do. Some men believe and speak boldly that a woman cannot raise a son without the help of a man, because there are too many things that only a man can teach a son. As a woman Pastor I have gotten the same argument that God never calls a woman to lead men, and that only a man can lead other men.

During Dalen's Junior High days I must admit I had no love or forgiveness in my heart for my husband. Secretly, I felt the same way Dalen did. Dalen was more honest with his feelings while I tried to hide mine because I was pastor of a church and week after week I stood before people encouraging them to love one another and forgive. I was trying to be all that God had called me to be to his people so their faith would not fail them.

Dalen always wanted to be on the go especially when his father was home. Any excuse would do for him to leave the house. He tried any and every sport that would get him to school early and bring him home late. If he wasn't involved in these types of activities, he wanted to be with his friends. I did not allow Dalen to spend a lot of time away from home at sleepovers unless they were close family members. I was still trying to protect him as I always had, however protecting a six or seven year old child is very different from trying to protect a twelve or thirteen year old pre-teen.

And then, like clockwork, Dalen's hormones kicked in and he knew he was no longer a little boy. Fathers, your sons desperately need you during this time in their lives to explain certain "male" things to them. They need you to help them understand the changes they feel in their bodies. Mothers, don't despair if there is no father in your son's life. This is the time you become very resourceful with God's help. Pray and ask God to send you the right male figure to help your son through.

Dalen
Me and My Wrong Friends

Since my mother was not the type of woman to spare the rod, I knew from an early age the difference between right and wrong. I was never the type of individual to hang around the wrong crowd, drink before age, or do drugs, but I did always want to have fun. I was pretty much willing to have fun at almost any cost. Although my parents were somewhat protective of me, they did allow a large window of freedom. With this new-found freedom I felt the need to find me some more new and exciting friends. Naturally I was drawn to kids who had been awarded far more freedom by their parents than I could ever dream of.

This was a point in my life where I was mesmerized by the glitz and glamour of a fast paced care-free lifestyle. Around the eighth grade I became friends with a boy on my basketball team by the name of Sam. Sam came from a family that seemed to give him any and everything he ever wanted. His fathered owned two franchised fast food chains. They drove nice cars. They had a two story house with a pool in the back. At the age of 13 I felt like that was the entire world. I would always ask my mother to drop me off over Sam's house. Every weekend I had to be spending time with Sam and his family. In my eyes, Sam had it all. Both of his parents were always home. His mother and his father were at all of our sporting events, and they let me and him go wherever he wanted to go. See Sam's parents didn't have the same rules as every other household. His mother would drop us off at the area teenage club; the same club that my parents had forbidden me to attend. His parents would allow us to stay out late at night, and have girls over all times of the day. This modern day Saddam and Gomorra instantly became my escape from reality. In the beginning my mother never really questioned me spending time with my friend and his family, until one weekend when everything changed.

It started off just as every other weekend did. I was released from school, took the bus home, and packed my bags. I was headed to my best friend's house. Just like our normal routine, my mother drove me to his parents' house, dropped me of and hugged me goodbye. I could tell by the smile on my friends face as I was walking into his house that this was not going to be an ordinary weekend and that he already had something up his sleeve. Dropping my bags down in his spare bedroom I just flat out asked him, "Man, what is the plan for this weekend?" Laughing, he began to tell me about this older girl he had met at the movie theatre a few weeks back that wanted her and her cousin to come pick us up and we spend the night with them. This was something entirely brand new to me. All I could do was laugh, and for him that was enough. Our plans were locked in. That evening, just as planned, the two young ladies pulled in front of my friends' house and honked the horn. Just as horses in the Kentucky Derby, once the door opened we were in a full out sprint. We hopped into the car with the two young ladies and excitedly embarked on a journey of a lifetime. Just like any two young teenagers plotting to stay out an entire night, we had no plan. Our quartet was wondering aimlessly around the city, but as long as we had a working vehicle and money in our pockets, we were good. As the hours slowly passed we began to run out of destinations, so we did the only thing we could think of; we went back to the young ladies' house. Once we had arrived, my friend and I paired up with our choice of the two ladies and went into separate bedrooms for the night.

Sometime around 1 in the morning I heard the ringing of the cell phone my mother had given me to keep in contact with her while I was away. Not knowing who it could possibly be calling me that late at night I picked up the phone only to see my home telephone number appearing on the screen. I could not for the life of me figure out why my mother was calling me this late. She had never done that before. Not wanting to be questioned and having to lie to my mother, I did what any other teenager would do, I refused to answer. After a few moments of back to back calling, they finally stopped, to only show the symbol for a newly received voicemail. As I began to listen to the voicemail my heart began to drop. On the other end of the phone all I heard was my mother pleading with me to call her back and just let her know that I was ok. I was nervous. I couldn't call her back for fear that I would be brutally chastised for lying and not being where I said I was going to be. My phone rang consistently throughout the entire night that I had to just cut it off. I was up bright and early the next morning terrified. The reality of the situation had finally set in. I was destined to be beaten for my actions. I pulled my friend to the side and the only plausible solution to our problem we thought, was to just man up and tell the truth and take our punishments. After mustering up enough courage I finally called my mother back. I don't think my wildest imagination could have had me prepared for what I heard on the other end of the receiver. I was expecting to be yelled at relentlessly, but all I heard was fear. I had never in my life heard my mother as terrified as she was at that moment. After hearing my voice for a few seconds and realizing I was ok, her terrified tone quickly shifted that of relief and anger. I had not realized that by not contacting my mother and being unreachable that entire night before that I had played on the worst fear a parent could ever have, losing their child. My mother had no clue what had happened to me. She didn't know if I was hurt, harmed, or even dead. Every possible worst case scenario was running through her mind that night. What was supposed to be a well plotted scheme of fun and mischief quickly turned into the worst nights' experience for my mother. The feeling alone of me knowing I caused so much grief to my mother was punishment enough. All I could do was apologize and tell the entire truth. To my amazement after returning home and finally seeing my mother, although mad, she didn't really punish me. I was expecting a beating of a lifetime; in turn I received something much worse. I was told by my mother how much I had disappointed her and let her down, and how she thought I was a better person than that. I was truly hurt. I had let down my number one fan, my best friend, my mother. I was devastated.

After a few days of somewhat eerie silence, my mother came to me and told me that we needed to talk. I was so happy that she wanted to talk to me again that I didn't care what the topic was. She sat me down just as she had done on many other occasions, and let out a long sigh. My mother began to explain to me the fear that I had caused her by my actions, and how no parent ever wants to feel that way in their lifetime. She then went on to talk to me about the quality of the people I chose to hang around, the people I called my friends. Apparently my mother had her reservations about my friend for a while now, but just chose not to say anything. Once this instance had taken place she felt that it was imperative for her to tell me her thoughts and opinions. My mother knew that I was very strong willed and would do whatever I was determined to do, and that all she could do is make suggestions to me with hopes that I took heed. She began to rationalize to me the importance of being honest and staying true to my conscience. She asked me at any point during my excursion did I feel like I was doing wrong. Of course I knew what I was doing was wrong but I went out of my way to try and rationalize it to myself. I tried to make myself believe that since I was with my friend at his house anything we did fell back on him with his parents and not mine. Stupid thought process, I know, so my mother explained to me that I should always follow my conscience. She always said that it was God quickening me to do what was right. She explained that not following your gut instinct or intuition could end up horribly, as it had for so many people before me. She went on to say that the glitz and glamour are okay, but children still need boundaries. She understood that she didn't allow me the same amount of freedom as some of my friends, but there was a method to what I thought was madness. She knew in the long run setting these boundaries and keeping me somewhat sheltered would keep me grounded and molded into a well respected gentleman some day. I must say, she knew what she was doing.

It is truly funny to me now, I sit back and look at all the friends that came through my life growing up, and it seems that all of the ones who said "Man, your mom is cool as hell, she lets you do whatever you want," are all in bad places in their lives right now. Unlike my wrong friends, I have graduated from college with two degrees, traveled the world, and most importantly, never been arrested. My mother ended our conversation with telling me something that her mother used to tell her, "You are the company that you keep." You should always surround yourself around people who are like minded and who are striving for upward positive motivation. She would say, "Friends are supposed to complement one another and heightened each other's existence, if someone is not ADDING to you they are just TAKING away from you." Boy was she right.

Part 5 – High School to College

Gwen

On a scale of one to ten, Dalen's and my experiences for him in high school were about an eight. He was enrolled in honor classes and met a new group of friends. His father and I were pleased with his new friends. They came from families who tried very hard to give their children healthy home environments. Most of the parents and their teenagers attended church, worked and supported their families. They attended their children's school activities. Still, our home continued to be the meeting place for Dalen and his friends.

Dalen was enrolled in a Driver's Ed course and began driving in the 10th grade. I was so fearful of riding with him but his father wasn't. His father was very adamant about Dalen's driving abilities and boldly stated how excellent of a driver his son was. Dalen got his first new car as a junior in high school. We didn't worry because he always obeyed our rules about the car.

Dalen's outside life was wonderful. He despised his home life but only when his father was under the same roof. If Dalen's father was home and I didn't allow Dalen to leave, he would stay in his room. He never asked his father for anything. He tried to talk with his father as little as possible and would only speak to him when he had to.

High school was very hard for me. I felt as though I was the meat between two slices of bread; Dalen and his father. They were eating me from both sides and seemed to be pulling on me simultaneously. There were days I felt I couldn't go on. The load and the pull were too great. I knew my duties to my husband but my love for my child caused me to be partial to him. I felt as if Dalen had been forced into this position and my husband chose his. He did not choose to make life better for himself or his family.

There were times Dalen would become upset with me because he felt betrayed when I would agree with his father about something that concerned him. I sometimes agreed because I knew my husband loved Dalen and would never willfully do anything to hurt him. I also knew that some of his life's experiences allowed him to know more about some things than Dalen and I did. As a result, I always went with wisdom rather than love. When Dalen was younger, I could tell him how much his father loved him but now he didn't want to hear it.

Dalen viewed love by what he saw in me. He knew beyond a shadow of a doubt I loved him and only wanted the best for him. My love was all he knew. His anger and resentment towards his father allowed his father's love for him to be smothered. It was as though cold water had been poured directly over a burning flame.

Dalen

Quentin Crisp once stated, "The young always have the same problem - how to rebel and conform at the same time. They have now solved this by defying their parents and copying one another." My high school career turned out to be a very huge eye opener. I was fresh out of a lifetime of shelter and false sense of comfort leaving private school, and thrown into the lion's den of the Dallas County public school system. This was an entire new lifestyle. Not only was this high school, it was my first real look at what I thought "real" kids looked and acted like. This was nothing like the robotic uniformed routine of my former private school matriculation. There were no more uniforms. No more Tuesday midday church services. No more corporal punishments. This was a lifestyle that I could quickly get adjusted to. And I did.

Ever since I tried to kiss Rosa Johnson under the playground slide in kindergarten, I knew I was going to be a ladies' man. Although I had high hopes for myself in this department, it was not until my freshman year of high school that the ladies actually started showing me any type of significant attention. I felt on top of the world. See, high school is a time in a young man's life that male guidance is not only really needed, but if not given can turn out truly detrimental to the youth's upbringing. This is a time when most young men start experimenting with sex, drugs, and alcohol. In a fatherless household, the task of explaining these things to the son will subsequently fall back on the mother. For that reason having an open line of communication is truly imperative. A pre-established relationship is mandatory between the mother and son by this point. The son must feel absolutely comfortable with his mother or he will turn to his friends to find out the answers to his questions, and that is the last thing as a parent you would ever want. One child teaching another about drugs, sex, and alcohol is about as productive and detrimental as the blind leading the blind.

What I respect most about my mother is that although she is a pastor of a church and a strong God fearing woman, she always kept it honest and truthful with me, not ever acting as if she was ever "holier than thou." My mother was never a drinker. I can honestly say that in my entire life I have only seen my mother take one sip of alcohol, and that was on vacation in the Virgin Islands while the host was making a toast. Since my mother never drank alcohol, we never kept any in the house. Without liquor being present in our home the temptation for me to drink was virtually nonexistent. I understand different people have different methods of getting the same point across. When it came to drinking, my aunt would allow my cousin to take small sips as a minor with hopes of it tainting her perspective on drinking once she got older. Her theory was correct. My cousin to this day genuinely cannot stand the taste of alcohol. Even though my mother took a different route than her sister, her method of not exposing me to liquor, but speaking on the consequences of drinking were very effective. It was not until I reached college that I had my first sip of alcohol.

When it came to drugs my mother would always stress the importance of staying as far away as possible. She made her point very clear by showing me the affects that drugs had on people. She would tell me stories of people she grew up with or people that I knew but was just too young to realize why they were the way they were or acted the way they acted. I asked my mother had she ever tried drugs before, she responded with pure honesty, she said she had tried marijuana once. The respect I had for my mother at that moment grew tremendously. My mother could have easily and without thinking twice have lied to me and I wouldn't have known anything different. For her to be honest with me just showed me a lot about the type of person she was and how serious this topic was to her. Just like any child, I wanted to know all about her experience. All I knew about my mother was she was an excellent person and a God fearing woman; I wanted to know about the rebellious Gwen. She went on to explain to me that she tried marijuana at a younger age and that she must have done it wrong because she encountered no effects from it. She said from that point she realized how pointless drugs were and never tried it again. With that story being told, at that age, the usage of drugs just didn't seem to intrigue me. Honestly, it was not until I heard a few fellow classmates of mine talking in the locker room about an incident that happened one weekend that my opinion of drugs became truly tainted. Apparently, a few guys from the basketball team were all at someone's house smoking marijuana, when one of the young guys pulled out a pistol that he had been carrying around with him the past few days.

It was not uncommon for guys at my high school to be carrying guns in their car or on their person. It seemed like around this age bracket everyone was trying to give off this pseudo-thug persona. Whether to impress the ladies, or to just seem tough, this thug mentality was running rapid through my school. So, as the guy was showing his friends the pistol, one boy took the gun and pretended to fire it a few times. By this time the entire group was beyond high. While the pistol was being passed around one way the lit blunt was being passed around the other way. As the blunt was being handed off it slipped from the finger tips of one of the guys and feel to the floor. At the exact moment of the guy bending down to pick up the marijuana, a loud BOOM echoed through the room as a speeding bullet flew right over his head and lodged into the wall directly behind him. High and not knowing, one of the guys had accidentally dislodged the safety and touched the hair pin trigger, firing the gun. It was only by the pure grace of God that no one was killed that day. After hearing that story I knew I didn't want to be a part of anything that was going to alter my senses in a way that would make me function in potentially harmful manner.

When it came down to the topic of sex, it would have been ideal to have the traditional father-son talk. Since my father was not around like he should have been, once again my mother had to step up to the plate. We never really just sat down and discussed the "birds and the bees," we just sort of had an open dialogue where she would explain to me what the Bible said about sex before marriage. One thing about my mother, she knew her son. My mother understood the type of person I was from an early age. She knew I was very strong willed and determined to make my own decisions. With that morsel of knowledge, my mother did her job by telling me about sex from a Christian standpoint, but also being 100% honest with me and explaining to me the importance of using condoms if I was going to have sex. Most parents would just teach and re-teach the importance of following what the Bible says about fornication and that's it, but what parents have to understand is, no matter what you teach or tell your child, temptation is out there and they will end up making their own decisions one way or another. It is much better for that child to be fully informed rather than be semi-informed and not taking the proper precautionary methods if their decision is not the one YOU had planned for them. With that being said, I quickly made my own decisions.

See, high school was a time in my life when I first started to notice and grow into my own unique character and personality. I was starting to become a tad bit more confident and a tad bit more rebellious. This was a time in my life where other kids my age had extreme freedom, and I surely was not going to be left out. This is a time in my life where I started to become bolder. I was more willing to take chances. This was a time that I started to understand that for every negative action there was going to be either an equal to or greater than negative consequence. At this age I was able to determine if the action I was scheming to participate in was worth the consequences that would soon follow. That is the wrong place for the mind of a teenager to be, not only for them, but for the parent as well. That state of mind is genuinely saying, "If need be, I am willing to deal with the punishment, because it is only temporary." So at the time of the punishment the child really hasn't learned his lesson, because he/she was already expecting the outcome. To them, the punishment was all a part of the grand scheme of things. My mother quickly caught on to this thought process when one day I lied to her. In my mind, I knew the consequence for lying was a whooping, so I was ready. For some reason, my mother switched it up on me. This time she knew there was a big party coming up a few weeks later that she knew I wanted to attend. In my mind that party was too far away to be affected by my actions. As the punishment for my wrong doing she told me I could not attend the event. I was livid. I began to ask her what happened to the whooping I was supposed to get. I began to try and barter the event for my beating. At that moment, my mother knew that in my head I had contrived this entire plan, from beginning to end, and that this curveball she threw really knocked me off my square. She knew that from that day forth she had to stay a few steps ahead of me at all times.

As my matriculation through high school officially got underway, I started to become more popular and more aware of my surroundings. By now I had started driving, which in turn opened up a brand new set of concerns. Once a teenager becomes mobile, the parents must in turn become more aware of their child's habits and conversations. Once I started driving, I started to pay close attention to my parent's daily habits. Just as much as my mother thought she was watching me, I was just as much doing the same to her. I had pin pointed the exact time my mother would be going to sleep, how many times throughout the night she usually woke up, and the exact time she would wake up for the morning. It was like clockwork. I had also constructed a pretty accurate schedule to when my father would be leaving and how many days it would be before he came back. The very few times my father was home and stayed the night with his family it was kind of hard to gauge his sleeping pattern. He would always be up and walking around at random times of the night, so for the most part all of my mischief took place when he wasn't home.

Having my mother's routine down to a science made it very easy for me to come and go as I pleased all throughout high school. It was if the only thing that occupied my mind at this age was GIRLS. I was obsessed, that's all I thought about. I would wait until my mother went to sleep and I would quietly sneak out of bed, get fully dressed, and without a second thought roll the car out of the garage and down the driveway and successfully drive off into the night. I would probably take the car three nights out of the week while my mother quietly slept. I would always end up at some girls' house sometimes 20-30 miles away. I was spontaneous. I never thought of the dangers that lurked in the night, I was more concerned with having fun and living life. It never failed; I would always come home just moments before my mother would wake up for the morning. Only a few hours after getting home from my night's journeys, I would be awakened by my mother to start getting ready for school. I would be dead tired throughout the entire school day. I would even find myself dozing off in class, but a slight scolding from an instructor was not enough to detour me from my night's plans. It is very ironic that I now sit back and recount my nightly activities and I notice how they subsequently paralleled those of my fathers. I guess indirectly his actions had a larger effect on me than I ever really noticed.

It's funny how God teaches you lessons in a way that scares you so much that it changes your whole outlook on situations, but doesn't allow harm to fall on you while proving his point. The joys and thrills of sneaking out of the house abruptly came to an end one night unexpectedly. I remember it as if it were seriously yesterday. I was asleep in my bed one Thursday night my senior year, with no intentions of sneaking out of the house, when I received a telephone call around 2:30 AM. Still in a deep daze, I answered the phone very groggily. On the other end of the receiver I heard the voice of one of the young ladies who I had occasionally snuck out of the house to go visit at times. She seemed very upset and shaken. She began to tell me that she was on a date with a guy who had put her out of his car and left her stranded at a gas station less than a mile from my house. She then asked me if I would please pick her up and take her home. Even though I was tired and knew she stayed about 40-45 minutes away from me, I felt this is the gentlemanly thing to do. So, I did a quick parental bedroom check and saw that my mother was deep into her sleep as usual, and quickly made my way to the car and down the driveway, just as I had perfected a thousand times before. A few seconds later I reach the gas station where the young lady was sitting on the curb waiting for me. She quickly jumped into the vehicle and gave me a huge hug thanking me for helping her out.

For the next 40 minutes on the way to her home we joked and talked and pretty much enjoyed each other's company. It was not until I pulled up in front of her house that things went totally south. I parked the car and waited for her to unbuckle her seat belt and exit the car. She didn't. In a joking manner, I explained to her that she had to go into her house so I could get home before my mother woke up. She refused. Calling her bluff I told her if she did not exit the vehicle she would be having a one way ride back to my side of town. She still refused. I quickly turned the car around began to drive away from her neighborhood. No sooner than we exited her main street did this young woman swing as hard as she could and punched me in the side of my face. I was astonished. I was livid. I was confused. I did not know how to respond to this sudden act of violence. All I could do at that exact moment was to ask her why in the HELL did she just do that. She swiftly responded with another punch to the side of my face. Not knowing what to do, I told her how crazy she was and sped back to her house. Once in front of her house for the second time, the nightmare only continued. She still would not get out of the car. I slammed the gear into park and cut off the ignition and got out of the car and walked over to the passenger side of the vehicle. I swung open her door with every ounce of anger I had in me and told her to get the HELL out of my car. And like clockwork, she refused. I was baffled. I did the only thing I could possibly think of, I reached into the car to unbuckle her seatbelt myself.

I learned how big of a mistake that was very quickly. No sooner than my hand touched the red "push" button on the seatbelt release mechanism, her balled up fist connected with my jaw with so much force that my head hit the dash board. As mad as I was, and as much as I wanted to hit her back, I restrained myself. I just kept hearing my mother's voice telling me that a man never puts his hands on a woman to harm her, only to love her. I wanted to love her alright; with the same amount of "love" she had just showed my jaw. Showing much restraint, I just grabbed her and physically picked her up out of the car and set her down on her feet. I then slammed the passenger door closed and bolted to the driver's side. As I was entering the driver's side of the vehicle she then dives head first into the car on top of me and began to rip at my shirt and trying to choke me. I mustered up all the strength I could and pushed her off of me and out of the car and slammed the door closed. I quickly started the car and began to drive off. As the car began to move this girl tried to jump on the hood of the car. I quickly stopped. She then tried to come to the driver's side door once again and I just pressed the gas as hard as I could and sped down the street in total shock.

Once I got a few miles from her house I pulled over to a gas station and just sat there in pure shock. My hands were shaking, my shirt was tore, my lip was bleeding, and I was genuinely scared. I then did the only thing that I could think to do at a time like that, I called my best friend and told him the story. He reassured me that as long as I didn't hit her or put my hands on her I would be ok. After that conversation I calmed down slightly. It wasn't until I was halfway home that my phone began to ring from a telephone number that I did not recognize. I answered only to hear the young lady's mother on the other end yelling and screaming at me. She began to ask me why I had beat up her daughter. I was floored! I had not hit this young lady at all. I began to tell this woman the whole story from start to finish and let her know how CRAZY her daughter was. She seemed to believe me but before she hung up she told me that her daughter was calling the police on me. I knew in my mind that I had done nothing wrong but I was terrified. I just knew that once I pulled up to the house there was going to be about 30 police cars in front waiting to arrest me. I prayed the entire rest of the way home. I made all types of promises to God. I told God that if he saved me from this situation I would never sneak out or anything like that ever in life. Needless to say, when I arrived home there were no police vehicles and my mother was still asleep. I pushed the car back into the garage and crawled back into my bed and just stared at the wall the remainder of the night. That was the last time I snuck out of my house. Needless to say, I never heard from the girl, her mother, or the police again.

As I grew a little older, and watched the hairs on my chin start to sprout sparsely, I felt on top of the world. My high school years were starting to wind down. With this false sense of adulthood came more aggression and more tension between my father and myself. I felt as though I was a man, that I was tough, that I could stand my own ground. I began to walk around my own home like I was the King of this castle and my father was just some mere peasant. I felt in my heart since he was never around there was nothing much he could say or do to me. Whenever he felt the need to come home and rest, change clothes, or grab a bite to eat it was a total war zone. Growing up learning about the Civil War as a child I could never wrap my mind around the idea of how brothers and fathers and uncles and cousins could wage war on one other just because they lived in two separate regions of our great country. As I grew older my mentality quickly changed. I understood fully how two individuals stemming from the same bloodline could harbor so much disdain for one another and be drawn to battle over extreme disagreements. Anytime my father felt the need to correct or discipline me it quickly turned into an argument and an all-out shouting battle. I had no respect for him and he knew it. He was losing me. The only person that could intervene with our battles was my mother. She would beg and plead with us both to stop fighting with one another. We would oblige her and stop our arguing and go our separate ways into separate rooms. These few moments of truce would quickly come crashing down once our paths crossed again. After a while I became fed up with the bickering and arguing myself, and found a new solution. I just ignored my father at all costs. I would walk into my house and speak to everyone in a room and walk right pass my father. I would go days at a time seeing my father and not speaking to him. We just genuinely had nothing to say to one another, and I liked it that way.

The tension in our household became so thick that it would literally drain the energy out of my mother. My mother, who loved both me and my father dearly, quickly became caught in the middle of our situations. At times the confusion in the household just became too much for my mother. With her trying to get her sermon ready for the following week, the stress we caused started to become a true detriment. My mother would beg and plead with me and my father to stop our bickering and arguing to no avail. My mother would have different family members come to me and pull me to the side to try and convince me to at least try and get along with my father. I was stubborn, and there was no way I was going to give in. I looked at the situation as, I will be graduating real soon and I will be on the first thing smoking to HOTLANTA, Georgia and then I would not ever have to deal with him again. My mind was made up. I had a plan, and I was determined to stick to it.

Gwen

Life became somewhat of a nightmare for Dalen and me during his senior year of high school. Up until now, Dalen had been a model student with good grades. I didn't worry about teachers calling me at home. I was so thankful God had kept His hand upon Dalen. He kept Dalen from drugs, alcohol and gangs, but then things changed. Dalen was a senior, this was his last year and it would be similar to his past three years - or so I thought. Teachers began calling me every day because Dalen was doing things in class he'd never done before. His grades began to drop. School was not important to him anymore and all he wanted to do was have fun. I was quite perplexed by his behavior.

Dalen's father was away working most of the time, so neither Dalen nor I could blame his behavior on my husband. Dalen was seventeen years old and had to be responsible for his own actions. I became frustrated with Dalen and couldn't for the life of me figure out what was going on with him. I was fairly certain it wasn't drugs. I prayed more for Dalen than I ever had. I called in several powerful intercessors to pray for him. Fear was all over me. Negative thoughts captured my mind telling me all kinds of lies about Dalen; lies such as he wouldn't finish high school, would never go to college or would end up like his father, having no control over his life. Something or someone was controlling Dalen.

Dalen's behavior spanned the entire first semester. The one positive thing that happened was when the three of us went to Atlanta, Georgia to visit Clark Atlanta University. Dalen was so excited! CAU was the only school he wanted to attend. It was a big source of support for me and Dalen when his father accompanied us. We were there four days and saw all CAU had to offer. My husband and I promised Dalen we would pray and do everything in our power to make his desire a reality. I really wanted Dalen to attend school in Texas because I wasn't ready for him to be so far away from me. He felt needed to mature just a little more.

The second semester of high school started the same as the first.

Dalen refused to follow the rules at school. He did what he wanted, when he wanted. Dalen had his first fight his senior year but I didn't share this with my husband. I knew if I had told him, he would have tried to be the father he should have been all along. Telling his father would have been an accident waiting to happen; a stick of dynamite waiting to explode.

Education has always been a major part of my husband's life. On a scale of 1-10, education was a 15 with him. The thought of Dalen causing trouble for teachers would have caused a World War III in our home, so I decided to remain quiet. I knew God had a ram in the bush. One random morning my niece called Dalen and to my surprise, his behavior had changed completely the next day. Just imagine it - one telephone call caused Dalen to transform into a young man. Until this day, I don't know all the details but I do know I cannot speak some of the words she spoke to him. Nevertheless, it worked and I thank God. Although I don't know the real reason behind Dalen's behavior, I would guess he was acting out his negative emotions towards his father.

Dalen

Towards my senior year of high school, school started to mean absolutely nothing to me. I was more concerned with working and chasing after girls. Around this time I was starting to gain a lot of attention from the ladies. I must say, I was feeling myself. It was as if nothing else mattered. I had stop paying attention in class. I was becoming disruptive. I was sleeping in class. I just did not care. It was not as if I was doing drugs or drinking or anything, but my vice was GIRLS. There was not a day that didn't go by my senior year without my teachers calling my house trying to speak to my mother. She didn't know what to do. I was seriously becoming rebellious, and for the most part, I just felt as though at 17 I was grown. I think back at it now and laugh at how naïve I was. After days, weeks, and months of trying to convince me to behave at school, focus in class, and get along with my father, I guess my mother had reached her max and had had enough. Her next move even surprised me. I woke up one morning just like any other day and got dressed and hopped in my car to drive to school. I was running a tad bit late as usual, but I really didn't care. No sooner than I pulled out of my driveway my cell phone began to ring. I looked down to saw that it was a telephone number that I did not recognize. Interested in seeing which girl was calling me this early in the morning, I eagerly answered. On the other end of the line I was quickly greeted with a loud and abrasive "What the HELL is your problem?!" That voice till this day still sends chills down my spine. The voice on the other end of the phone was one that I quickly recognized. It was my older cousin Tasha, who along with my cousin Kendra had acted as surrogate mothers to me. Stunned, I asked what do you mean, and at that exact moment I received the cursing out of a lifetime. One so bad that till this day I still think about it and get a little nervous. My cousin Tasha began to talk to me holding back no expletives. She began to tell me how tired she was of hearing my mother complain about my behavior, attitude, performance at school, and relationship with my father. She told me that if I did not straighten up immediately that she would "beat the black off my ass."

The crazy thing is, as tough as I thought I was, I knew she was a woman of her word and if she said it then she meant it. Besides, Tasha was and still is notorious for her disciplinarian techniques. She began to explain to me the hurt and grief that I was causing my mother, while putting everything else into perspective. She shed a huge light on the nature of girls and how I was allowing them to control and overpower my routine. She enlightened me to the fact that as much as I was chasing after these girls and slacking off in my studies and responsibilities, that I better believe that they were doing the exact opposite. She went on to explain that the majority of women are excellent multi-taskers and as much as I think they are giving me their whole attention, I better quickly understand that they are getting their work done and that their grades weren't dropping like mine. Women will always be around, is what she kept repeating, and that I needed to focus and what I needed to do with my education first then have fun later. It genuinely made sense. Who would have thought that all I needed was a cursing out by someone who truly cared about my well being? I went home that evening with a whole new outlook. I told my mother about the conversation I had earlier and sincerely apologized for my actions. From that day forth I straightened up. Although I didn't fully put my differences aside with my father, I did become more cordial for my mother's sake, and she was appreciative.

As the days went on, I watched as my high school matriculation wound down. What seemed so much like yesterday, with me ironing my clothes for the first day of class my freshman year, quickly turned into a mad dash to get ready for my senior prom almost four years later. Senior prom was a very important time for me. This was one night that my mother set aside a few of her rules, including curfew, and just allowed me to have fun. It was my first real taste of "adulthood" and I was ecstatic! What started off as the best time of my life thus far leading up to the prom almost turned into a huge disappointment. Amidst all the excitement surrounding getting ready for prom, the finding the date, hotel, and vehicle, I quickly realized I knew nothing about men's fashion, or even how to tie a tie. In my eyes, there was no task too great for my mother. I went to her with a sincere look in my eye and explained to her my concerns, and as usual she stepped up to the plate. With my father not being around, my mother and I sat there for about an hour and tried to teach ourselves how to properly tie a necktie, but to no avail. My mother finally called for reinforcements. Within minutes my cousin Kendra was walking into our home ready to get the show underway. Kendra gave me a quick style rundown and sat there and taught me and my mother how to tie a necktie within a few seconds. After my fashion lessons were complete, it was time for the two ladies to give me my gentleman rundown. We briefly touched on all aspects of making sure that I upheld myself as the true southern gentleman that they had raised me to be. We went over everything from opening all doors for my date to me standing up when she entered the room. That 3 hour crash course had me ready to take over the world. Thanks to those two women, prom was everything I had hoped and dreamed of. After prom a few days later came graduation. I had cleaned up my act, and my family was excited to see me make that journey into college. Everyone showed up and showed out to the festivities, even my father. I was a high school graduate and college bound. There was nothing that was going to keep me from Atlanta, Georgia, and I meant nothing.

Gwen

This book is not about emotions; yet I feel compelled to discuss them briefly to help readers of this book understand and deal more effectively with children who are experiencing different emotions. Everyone has moments in their life when emotions get out of control. It is not unusual to encounter circumstances in life that cause us to be frustrated, sad, or even angry. We also encounter positive things that cause our emotions to soar. The key is to refuse to allow your life and the decisions you make to be ruled by your emotions…good or bad. Emotions aren't bad but are generally caused by pain or pleasure. They are designed to move you in a certain direction, either toward something or away from it. Our ability to experience emotions is a gift from God. When you allow emotions to control you, you continually make decisions that are detrimental to your future and perhaps your own children. Dalen's emotions were detrimental to his future. Proverbs 23:7 says, "For as he thinketh in his heart, so is he." The way you think determines the course of your life, and your thinking is framed by the words you hear or speak.

If you associate with people who speak words of anger and resentment, don't be surprised if you find it hard to say something good about someone who has caused you hurt or pain over a long period of time. Your words produce thinking, and thinking produces feelings and emotions which produce decisions. Negative decisions produce actions which produce habits, which in turn produce character. Character leads you to your destination. When emotions spin out of control, they can cause tremendous damage to us and others. Depression, anxiety, and fear are some of the emotions that can definitely cause us damage. When these emotions begin to operate in our lives or our children's lives we begin to experience temptation. Temptation is pressure applied to our flesh that impacts our thinking and moves us away from where we should be. The root of most negative emotions is actually a powerlessness to do anything that would or could cause change on your behalf. As a believer and a woman of faith and prayer, I have found nothing that cannot be made better through the word of God.

Beginning in Dalen's Junior High years, I asked God to give me a keen eye to watch over Dalen and observe the things he did or didn't do. I wanted to know the emotions that were trying to manifest in his behavior. I knew he had dealt with hurt most of his life because of the lack of his father's presence in his day-to-day life. I felt the deep need to become watchful for other traits. Once we experience a deep hurt that is not dealt with over a long period of time, we may become depressed. One word to the wise; the ability to quickly dismiss things people do to hurt you will likely cause you to live free of anger and depression. What matters most is how you respond to challenges when they arise.

The most painful hurt one can experience is being hurt by someone you love. When that happens and you don't allow yourself to be healed or freed from this pain, rejection will set in. You must never allow yourself or your child to submit to rejection. You must stay above rejection and refuse to allow wrong thoughts to linger in your mind. As parents, we play a big role in keeping our children free of rejection. To do so, we must first be willing ourselves to forgive in order to move forward to a happy and healthy life.

It took years for Dalen to forgive his father. I must admit there were times I felt as if it would never happen. How do you begin to forgive someone who has hurt you when the back of them walking away from you looks better than the front of them coming towards you? Dalen felt this way 100% of the time and truthfully, I felt that way 95% of the time. Remember, if you don't deal with those things that have hurt you or your child, neither of you will be able to reach your final destiny without causing pain to someone else. People who hurt, hurt others.

Finally, allow me to touch upon anger. We've all experienced it, and likely acted out negatively as a result. Anger itself is not necessarily bad, but how it's directed can be the issue. There are people who are in prison right now because their anger prompted them to commit a crime. They likely acted in haste because they let the anger fester. Anger is the one emotion that can carry you on a trip you didn't even purchase a ticket for. Anger makes you want to get even. There is no such thing as getting even. You simply allow what happens to you to cause you to contemplate doing something that will escalate your life so far out of control that you regret the day you gave into the emotion.

Parents and children are much more vulnerable to a lifetime of hardship when anger is at the very root of your every being. Anger does not have to control you or your child. The choice is yours. If you or your child want to change how you feel, you've got to change how you think. Once again, remember the word of God says in Proverbs 23:7, "For as man thinketh in his heart, so is he."

Dalen
The Collegiate Years

All throughout high school I was determined to move out of Dallas and go to an out of state college. With my relationship with my father being as rocky as it was, I just felt the need to leave and get away as far as I could and start a life on my own. I knew it would be kind of hard to be away from my mother, but this was a step I had to take for my own betterment. It was funny because I only applied to one college, Clark Atlanta University. I applied for early admission and was granted early acceptance with a full academic scholarship. I quickly accepted. All it took was for me to visit the campus one time and to see all the beautiful women there, and I was completely sold. There were no more questions in my mind to where I needed to be.

Although very cliché sounding, I can honestly say that college was genuinely the best years of my life, at least thus far. It truly amazes me to think how much I matured throughout my collegiate matriculation. I watched myself turn from a mere boy into an accomplished man over a few significant years. With the years passing, it seemed as if I and my mother's relationship grew that much stronger. I can honestly say that while in college I did not let one day go by without my mother hearing my voice. Some days we would even speak two to three times. With all the effort I put into keeping in touch with my mother and keeping her up to date with my well being, I put the same amount of energy into not doing the same with my father. It is kind of weird, but I found myself going out my way to NOT speak to my father. I would know my mother's schedule front to back so I wouldn't slip up and call the house when she was not there and be indirectly forced to speak to my father when he answered the telephone. I even went to the extent of never saving, nor memorizing my father's cell phone number because I knew that sense I had been in college I had not answered calls from telephone numbers I did not recognize.

For some reason it truly bothered my mother that I never spoke to my father. I would go months at a time not speaking to him over the telephone. My mother would be standing right in front of my father and ask me would I like to speak with him, I would politely decline and tell her I loved her and would call her tomorrow. I just truly felt that since me and my father didn't have a strong relationship all the while we were in the same state, city, and at times household, there was no point in faking the funk and trying to hold onto something that was never there to begin with. Like clockwork, it never failed - my mother would call me once a week, and like a broken record would ask me the same question over and over again; "Dalen, have you talked to your father?" You would think after me telling her no and changing the subject shortly thereafter she would have sooner or later given up. Not my mother. She was on a mission. She was determined to mend me and my father's relationship one way or another. Remember, I came from this woman's womb, therefore she knows everything about me. My mother knows what I am thinking before I even think it; at least that is what she used to tell me when I was a child. It wasn't until one specific conversation that I will never forget that my mother truly showed me the importance of me talking to my father. The conversation started off normal as usual. We spoke about the same topics we always did, school, friends, and if I needed anything. Right as we were about to say our goodbyes she once again asked me had I spoke to my father lately, and like usual I said no. Before I could change the subject and tell her I would talk to her tomorrow she said, "Look Dalen, I'll pay you to call your father." I responded with, "Excuse me?" She replied, "You heard me, I will pay you to call your father once a week." At that moment it felt as if a ton of bricks had been dropped on top of me. I can remember thinking to myself that if this woman that means the world to me is willing to pay me just to talk to my father, then this must be very serious and dear to her. I knew she had been trying to mend me and my father's relationship for some years now, but I didn't think she would ever go to the extreme of paying me. After a brief silence I told my mother that she would never have to pay me to do ANYTHING for her and if that is what she wanted me to do then I would do it, for her. From then on out, I am not going to lie, I still didn't call him, but I did talk to him from time to time when I would call home to speak to my mother.

As my college years went on, I actually felt myself truly maturing. I was doing way better in college than I had ever done in high school. My grades were excellent, my relationships with professors we fantastic, and the group of friends I had chosen couldn't be any better. I guess that talk from my cousin Tasha actually went a lot further than I thought.

After a few years of hard work it came time for me to start considering if I was going to pledge a fraternity or not. All I knew growing up was Alpha Phi Alpha, Fraternity Inc., because my father, cousins, and uncles were all members. Growing up I was raised into believing I was going to become an Alpha Man, but growing up with such a rocky relationship with my father, I at times wanted to distance myself as much as possible from him. With that being said, when it came down to me researching the different fraternities my school had to offer, I was quickly drawn to Kappa Alpha Psi Fraternity, Inc. What interested me the most about fraternities were the camaraderie and brotherhood that they offered to young guys like me. Coming from a household where I was an only child, this ideology was phenomenal. Having committed to the process, I jumped in head first. I can truthfully say that the entire pledge process taught me a lot about myself as an individual. It opened me up to a lot of emotions and strengths that I never even knew I possessed. I was able to look at certain situations in different lights all of a sudden. One of the situations I reevaluated was my relationship with my father. Up until this time in my life I was in denial. I tried to make myself believe that I just really didn't care about our relationship. I fooled myself into believing that it just didn't matter and that I was genuinely not affected by it. It was not until one sleepless night during my pledge process that I began to think. I was all of a sudden hit by a wall of emotions that I had never felt before. I began to recall certain instances in my childhood that hadn't really bothered me then but made me realize that I still held them hostage in the back of my mind. Memories of the missed father son camping trip, thoughts of being called boy, recollection of the arguments and fights, all came rushing through my mind as if someone had opened the flood gates. And at that exact moment I realized that I was harboring a ton of animosity towards my father. It wasn't until that exact moment that I realized that I was just as much of the problem and it was not all my father's fault. As long as I held these feelings and emotions captive in my heart and soul, my father and I would never have a healthy relationship. Needless to say, although I had this epiphany, I still didn't act on it. I was stubborn. I just wasn't ready. The days went by and my pledge process wound on down. When it came time for me to be introduced to the world as a Man of Kappa Alpha Psi, Fraternity Inc., my mother hopped on the first flight to Atlanta and was in the front row supporting her son. If no one else was there, it was enough to see the smile on my mother's face. She was proud of her son, her baby, her now Kappa Man.

As my matriculation through Clark Atlanta University came to an end, I found myself about to graduate with honors. I just knew my mother would be proud. Everyone showed up to my gradation, my entire family. They all came out in droves, even my father. After my graduation reception, my father pulled me to the side, hugged me, and told me how proud he was of me. For that brief second I let my wall of disdain down, and we were a happy family.

My Guardian Angel

Attending college and living life in Atlanta, Georgia provided for a rollercoaster of wild and crazy times. Matter of fact, they were some of the best times I have yet to experience. I met a lot of great people and experienced a lot monumental things. I was able to experience everything from pledging a Divine 9 organization to meeting influential leaders to even attending Mrs. Coretta Scott King's funeral. Out of all my experiences in Atlanta, I can honestly say that the strangest and most life altering experience that ever happened to me took place right before I graduated from undergrad. Both my mother and father were in town for a ceremony where I was being inducted into Beta Gamma Sigma, an international business honor society. One night while my mother and father were asleep in their hotel room, I decided to go out for a night on the town with a few of my fraternity brothers. Usually when I went out I typically dressed up with a nice tie and blazer or a crisp pair of slacks. But for some odd reason this night I just didn't feel like getting dressed. I hurried along and threw on a nice pair of denim and a classic shirt; still looking dapper I might add. After meeting up with my fraternity brothers I realized that everyone else had on slacks except me and a friend. This was a total role reversal from the norm. Nonetheless we left for the lounge we were going to that night. Once we arrived we found out that this specific night the establishment was enforcing a strict dress code policy. No jeans allowed! I was floored. The one night I chose to dress down I would not be admitted into the party. I just figured maybe it wasn't meant for me to be out that particular night and told my friends to go ahead and go in and I would just go home because I was tired anyway.

As I walking away heading toward my car my friend who also chose not to meet the dress requirements for the evening jogged up to me and asked me if I would mind dropping him off at this other party downtown on my way home. Since I was headed that way anyway I politely obliged. On the way to the party my friend kept trying to convince me to just come to the party with him. He told me that I wouldn't have to pay for anything the entire night. By the end of the ride my friend had successfully convinced me to go inside the party with him. Parking downtown seemed to be ridiculous this particular night. We had to park all the way at a meter a few blocks away from the venue where the party was being held. As we began to walk to the venue I just kept getting a strange feeling that was altering my decision to go into the party. I tried my hardest to not think about this quickening in my soul and just kept walking with my friend all the way to the line to get into the party. Once I saw how long the line was I figured this was the perfect opportunity to use for me to not go into the party. I guess my friend saw the look in my face and before I could even say anything he spoke up and said, "Don't worry bro, I just sent my friend a text and he is going to meet us at the door. We are not about to wait in this line!" All I could think to myself was damn, now what can I use as an excuse not to go into this club.

After debating it over for a few seconds in my mind I just decided to tell the truth and just go home. I turned around to my friend and told him to just go in without me, and that I was just going to go ahead and head home and rest tonight. He understood. I stood there for a moment and watched to make sure that he made it in before I left him there stranded. Sure enough his friend came to the door and ushered him into the party; proudly skipping the line I might add. As I was turning around to walk away a group of 3 gorgeous young women walked past me and asked me was I going to come inside the party? For a brief second I contemplated changing my mind. I just shrugged my shoulders and told the ladies, "not this time." After exchanging a few flirtatious laughs I turned to walk away once more. As I was turning around, not paying attention I accidentally bumped into a tall skinny white guy who obviously wasn't paying attention either. We both apologized and made sure the other was ok. I reached my hand out to solidify our good standings when he began to introduce himself, "Hey buddy, I'm Shawn, a bartender here. You want to come in? You can walk in with me." I politely declined the offer and started walking again. As I was walking I began to think. I couldn't for the life of me understand why so many different people were trying to get me to go inside this party. I was desperately trying to convince myself to turn around and just go inside before I missed out on something crazy. As I was walking deep in thought a homeless gentleman approached me and asked me did I have any spare change. I politely told him no. I lied. Now don't get me wrong, on some occasions I feel compelled to share with the homeless, but this time while deep in thought, that was the last thing on my mind. I watched the homeless guy walk away and interrupt the conversation a few young college students and asked them for any spare change. Unlike myself, instead of giving this guy a polite no, these ignorant "children" began to curse him out and proceeded to tell him how dirty and worthless he was. Like a dog with his tail between his legs, he quickly scurried away. Seeing homeless people treated that way was nothing new to me in Atlanta, so I just kept moving.

After a few moments of walking at a slow pace still in deep thought I noticed that I had caught up with the homeless gentleman and found him digging through a trashcan. As I walked passed him something inside of me urged me to speak and apologize on behalf of the rude students earlier. He looked up with a slight smile on his face and politely accepted my apology and quietly returned to searching through the garbage can. I felt my job was done, and continued to walk away. Boy was I EVER wrong. After about 30 steps and reaching a crosswalk waiting on the light to change I heard footsteps running up behind me. I turned around startled; only to find the same homeless gentleman standing there with what seemed to be a plastic container of rice that he pulled from his hunt through the trash. Before I could even say anything to the guy he spoke to me, "You know, I didn't always use to be like this." For some reason these words touched my soul and I became truly intrigued and wanted to hear his story. I then asked with a look of sincerity, "What did your life used to be like?" He eagerly began to tell me of a life he once lived. He had been a star basketball player in high school and went on to get a full basketball scholarship to Morris Brown College. He told me that while attending Morris Brown College, he had all the girls, all the money, and all the jewelry he could ever want. He then went on to tell me how his brother was some huge doctor in Atlanta and his sister had done some type of work on Hartsfield International Airport there in Atlanta, and how he was the only one in his family to fall victim of this lifestyle. At this point I just listened. Sometimes all it takes is for you to just listen. Although I so desperately wanted to ask him what happened in his life that drove him to this current lifestyle, I didn't. I just listened. As he was talking and eating his meal another homeless guy walked up to us, and without any words being exchanged the homeless gentleman I was listening to broke the container of rice in half and gave one side of the rice to this man. The look in the man's eyes that received the meal was priceless. To me, it was reminiscent of Jesus breaking bread with his disciples. I just watched and listened in amazement.

After the exchange was over and the other homeless guy had walked away the gentleman looked over at me and asked me my name. I replied with, "Dalen." To my surprise he responded with, "Well Dalen, do you mind if I walk with you to your car?" For some reason I felt no fear. No discomfort. No reason for me to tell him no. I looked at him and said, "That's fine, I'm parked a few blocks down." As we began to walk together the gentleman looked up at me and said, "You know Dalen, when I first became homeless, God had to really humble me. I was starving and refused to beg or eat out of a trash can. All I could do was pray. I would get down on my knees and just look up at the sky and with tears dripping down my face; I would just beg God to send me the smallest bit of food. And right when I felt like I was at my end, two women came outside of a restaurant carrying to go bags. Just as one went to open the trash can and place it in, something changed her mind and she closed the lid and placed her meal on top of the trash can. As her and her friend walked away all I could do was start crying. I ran over the trash can and grabbed the food and began to eat. I thanked God with every bite I took. But Dalen, the amazing part was that as I was eating and praising God, with every bite I took it seemed as if more food was being added to the container. I ate until I was full. After I finished I looked into my container only to notice that it was still full and looked as if I never even took one bite. At that moment I knew it was God, and I felt the need to be a blessing to someone else. Not long after, I saw another homeless guy who seemed to have no shame ravishing through a trash can searching for his next meal. I kindly walked up to that brother and handed him my plate. I told him God had blessed me with it and now I am passing this blessing along to him, with the only condition being once he was finished he must pass it along to someone else who needed it. The guy being ever so grateful thanked God, and quickly obliged. Man Dalen, I know with everything in me that that container is somewhere in California right now still feeding people."

After hearing that story I was truly speechless. I didn't know what to say or how to react, and for some reason I most certainly believed him. The story was so touching it was hard for me to fight back the emotions. By this time we were walking up to my car, and for some reason I was being compelled to do something. Without even thinking I reached inside my pocket and gave the homeless gentleman every bit of money I had on me. It was almost $100. The homeless gentleman accepted the money without even counting it. He gazed up at me with such a look of gratitude that I understood how much of a blessing I had been to him, without words even being spoken. As I was about to get into my car the gentleman looked at me and asked me if I minded him giving me a hug. Without event thinking, or looking at how dirty his clothes were, I reached out my arms for an embrace. He gave me a true heartfelt hug. I honestly think that hug meant more to me than it did to him. After the hug he turned and walked away. After about five steps he turned around and said something to me that I will never in my life forget. He said, "Dalen, you are a business man." He then pointed up toward a high rise building and said, "One day you are going to have you one of those fortune 500 companies, and the next time you see me I am going to be dressed real nice, you won't even recognize me." I smiled and said thank you as he was walking off. Then he stopped once more and looked over his shoulder and said, "Oh yeah, Dalen, tell your mom Mike said hi. She will know who I am. Trust me." I didn't think much of it, I just said "ok," and got in my car and drove away. Now this is where the story gets kind of crazy. The next morning my mother took me and my fraternity brother to breakfast. And while we were eating and talking I began to tell my mother the entire story from the previous night. As the words were rolling off my tongue I began to see my mother's facial expressions slowly changing. With every word I spoke she seemed to become more engulfed into my story. As I reached the end of my night's tale and told her how I emptied the contents of pockets and gave it to the homeless gentleman, she seemed to be happy. She asked me about how much money do I think I gave him. I responded with, "Probably almost close to $100, but yeah momma as he was walking away he told me I was going to be successful and have a Fortune 500 company and everything. And he also told me to tell you that Mike said hi and that you would know who he was." For some reason I laughed when I told her that part of the story. I and my fraternity brother laughed. No sooner as the words rolled out of my mouth my mother began to cry. I had no clue of what to do or say. Million and one things were running through my mind at this exact moment. It even crossed my mind that "Mike" was possibly my biological father. My mind was racing from one extreme to the other. I finally asked my mother what was wrong and why was she crying. She responded with, "Mike, as in Michael. The angel Michael, why do you think he told you the next time you see him he will be in nice clothes and you won't even recognize him? Why do you think he told you to tell me he said hi and not your father? Why do you think he said I would know who he was? He was the Angel Michael and you passed your test." At that moment tears rolled down my eyes as well as my mothers. I was truly touched.

Whenever times get tough or I am not sure if I am on the right path in my life, I think about this story and it just reaffirms my motivation. This is one instance I will truly never forget. And like that plate of never ending rice, I pray that my story can be passed along to the masses, and inspire dedication and goodwill into the lives of others.

Out With the Truth

It sometimes seems that when you are high on life and you feel like things are going great, the world has a way of throwing you a curveball bringing you right back down to reality. In situations like these, one should always remember, the difference between a strike and a homerun is the amount of focus, will, and effort you choose to commit. I will never forget where I was at the exact moment I found out about two life changing events, the attack on 9/11 and me finding out my father was on drugs. Unlike being surrounded by teachers and other concerned students my age in the safe confines of my high school, when I found about my father I was 700 miles away from Dallas in Atlanta, Ga. driving down the street reading an email sent to my phone from my half sister. Who would have guessed a simple trip to Wendy's would unlock a closet full of skeletons. It was beyond my comprehension and understanding, the fact that my father was a drug addict. Warren Bennis once said, "We have more information now than we can use, and less knowledge and understanding than we need. Indeed, we seem to collect information because we have the ability to do so, but we are so busy collecting it that we haven't devised a means of using it. The true measure of any society is not what it knows but what it does with what it knows." The information I had just received left me dumbfounded. I didn't know what to do with this morsel of uninhibited truth that was thrown in my lap. Did I call my mother? Did I call my sister? Did I keep it to myself and act like it was all a bad dream? I did the only thing I could possibly do at that moment; I laughed. Now don't read this and automatically assume that I am crazy or heartless. It wasn't your typical slap of the knee laughter but more of the nervous you have to be kidding me smirk. This had to be a joke.

Allow me to back up a tad bit and speak on me and my sisters' relationship. We both share the same father and have a huge gap in our age. We have never lived in the same household and did not grow up together. We are very cordial but up until this point we never really held a lot of in depth conversations. For her to take the time to tell me something this serious about our dad, it had to have been true. I mean, we never play around with one another so I know her first joke wouldn't be something of this magnitude.

After a few emails back and forth between me and my sister more and more information was brought to light. She started to tell me how she was 21 years old when she first found out about our father's drug addiction, and that was the reason why she did not come around that often. She just couldn't bring herself to face this man. In her eyes he was full of lies and deceit. She then began to tell me how my mother spent my entire life shielding me from this demon. I was floored. As intelligent as I thought I was, I could not wrap my mind around the fact that my entire family knew about this deception but kept it a secret form me. I felt betrayed by the people I loved the most. She then went on to share with me that she had always felt growing up that our father just didn't like her, and once she found out about his addiction she understood his attitude and moodiness. This was a side of my sister that I had never seen before. She was opening up to me on a level that I would have never imagined possible. The thing that stood out the most about our conversation was that I could relate to every word she was saying. It had been times in my life that I felt like my father just didn't like me either. I can remember one specific argument that I had with my father when I was much younger. I had to have been about eleven or twelve years old. He made me so mad that I went into my room and slammed the door. Growing up in my parents' house there was one thing I knew I was never supposed to do, and that was closing my bedroom door. The sound of the door slamming behind me even startled me. For a brief second I could not believe that I had allowed myself to get that angry. At that exact moment I could only do one thing; count down the seconds until my father burst into the room. No sooner than I got down to 1 in my mind the door swung open and my father barged in yelling relentlessly. I didn't even have it in me to argue anymore. I just let him continue to scold me. After what seemed like an eternity of yelling he could tell by the look in my eyes that I was pondering something very deep. He then asked me, "What do you have to say for yourself boy?" At the tender age of eleven I mustered up enough courage and looked him dead in his eye and told him, "Once I grow up and move out this house I will NEVER in my life come back and see you. I don't ever want to see you again.

I understand why your daughter never comes back to visit and I don't blame her. The only person I will ever come back for is my mother!" I know it wasn't much, but I said it with so much faith and conviction that it kind of startled him. At that exact moment, as the words were coming out of my mouth, I saw my father's heart explode. I could see it in his eyes. His whole facial expression changed. At that moment I had found something that truly hurt him, and I knew it. At that exact instance I was the victor. I had won! I was able to make him feel the same way he had made me feel so many times before - worthless. All he did was stare at me for a few seconds while holding back the urge to shed a tear. I had to stand strong. I wouldn't apologize. I couldn't apologize. At that moment I meant what I said and there was no turning back. My father saw the dedication to my statement deep into my eyes. It was as if he was looking into my soul to find a different answer. He could look as deep and as long as he wanted, but there was nothing left. At that instant I had given him the real truth. It was a child and his purest honesty. All he could do was leave the room. I watched my father slowly walk away as if he had lost his best friend. And at that exact second, he had.

After finding out about my father's addiction certain things just started to make more sense. At least now I knew that it wasn't me that was the problem, and it wasn't that my father just didn't like me. In sort of a twisted way, I felt a tad bit better knowing that the reason he was so moody was because of these mind altering substances he was abusing. Now I needed to speak to my mother. I called my mother and brought my new found information to her attention. In a real calm voice she just went on to tell me that it was something she had known for a long time now but she just wanted to keep me away from it. She always felt that I was too young to know the truth about my father. Even though I was upset, I could respect her decision. Growing up I didn't need to know about my father's addiction, it wasn't my place. I found out about it at the most opportune moment for myself. We began to discuss the severity of the matter and came to the conclusion that all we can do is pray and leave it up to our Heavenly Father. And we did.

Being around my father after finding out about the news was at first kind of weird but I quickly got over it. I always wondered if he knew that I knew what his problem was? I wondered if he was ashamed? Was he remorseful? Did he have any regrets? And, why couldn't he just take the proper steps and procedures to get clean. From that day forth whenever I was home I would watch my father closely, and every time he left the house I wondered if he was out living his horrid lifestyle. I honestly kind of lost a little respect for him. Although very wrong of me, I felt like he couldn't tell me ANYTHING, especially when he had the type of problems he had. I felt like I had a better shot taking advice and criticism from myself, let alone a drug addict.

My Thoughts

After finding out about my father's drug addiction I began to look at the world differently. I began to question everything anyone had ever told me. I just could not understand how someone who was supposed to be held in such high regard as someone's father could be so hypocritical. It floored me when I thought about how this man could spend my entire life telling me what not to do and what to stay away from, when behind closed doors he was deeply engulfed in the exact same sinful underworld that he so adamantly preached against. As I sat and pondered these thoughts a while a new emotion started to arise; anger. I felt betrayed. For some reason I felt my entire life was based around this family secret, this family lie. Maybe it was selfish of me to feel the way I felt and not be concerned about my fathers' welfare, but I could not help it.

After hearing this momentous news, it was as if the tad bit of respect that I did have for my father was quickly thrown out the window. I didn't want to have anything to do with him. I didn't want him to ever correct or chastise me again. I felt that he had no room for judgment or critique.

I sincerely felt as though I was in a better place in my life than he could ever be. It was almost as if all of his accomplishments meant nothing to me anymore. I didn't care that he graduated from his high school in a class of one. I could care less that he went to one of the top medical schools in the country. I didn't think twice about him actually working as a rocket scientist. It meant nothing to me that he had opened up his very own medical practice and had done so much for the people in the surrounding communities that had no one else. All I could care about was myself and how I felt.

After speaking more with my mother I came to the realization that his problem was out of his realm of control. It was an addiction, and just like any other addiction it takes love and support to get through it. I had to mature quickly and get out of my selfish attitude and become more selfless. I had to set aside my anger toward my father for the greater good of the situation. The Hindu Prince Gautama Siddharta once proclaimed, "Anger will never disappear so long as thoughts of resentment are cherished in the mind. Anger will disappear just as soon as thoughts of resentment are forgotten." For me, forgetting was going to be the hard part. All I could do was pray and ask God to help me cleanse my heart from all ill emotions I had against my father, because I knew that was the only person that could pull me out of that funk. With time and prayer, I knew my anger would eventually turn into a different emotion, extreme concern. I would eventually begin to realize that what my father was doing to himself was becoming very detrimental to his life. No matter how much we fought and argued or how much I didn't respect him at times, I'd never wish death on him. I wanted him to get better, if not for me and our relationship, I at least felt as if he owed it to my mother for all the grief and hardships he caused her over the years. For practically being abandoned and forced to step up to a role without any prerequisites, my mother was required to quickly adjust and hit the ground running. She adjusted well to the role of a father teaching me lessons that helped guide me into the man I am today.

Part 6 – Dalen
Lessons My Mother Taught Me

Growing up around all women, and being raised by my mother, grandmother, aunts, and female cousins, I was able to get an inside scoop on how women operated. For a lack of better terms, I would almost compare it to "insider trading." For as long as I can remember my mother has always taken me to the side and explained to me how a REAL man should treat a woman. I did not know at that time but she was speaking based around her own life experiences. It still amazes me to this day how I live my life based on the lessons taught to me by my mother. Her lessons ranged all the way from how to treat a woman to how to run my household when I get married. I feel as if it is only necessary that I share a few of these lessons.

Lesson #1

The first and probably the most important lesson my mother ever taught me was to *never put my hands on a woman other than to show her love and affection*. She explained to me at an early age that her first husband was very abusive and physically hurt her. She began to tell me that only a coward puts his hands on a woman and that it takes a real man to walk away from a potential altercation. The conversation became undeniably real once I saw the look on my mother's face when she spoke of her first husbands' abusive nature. At that moment I knew that I never wanted to make any woman feel the way that that coward made my mother feel at that point in her life. I respect my mother tremendously for explaining to me at such an early age about her past life with her ex.

Although I was young, I was able to understand. I may not have been able to fully understand the magnitude of the situation in the first or second grade but I did know whatever happened hurt my mother and that was something that even at a an early age I knew wasn't right. From then on I knew that I never wanted to make any woman feel the way my mother felt when she was trapped in that tremulous relationship.

> *"Woman was taken out of man; not out of his head to top him, nor out of his feet to be trampled underfoot; but out of his side to be equal to him, under his arm to be protected, and near his heart to be loved."*
> *- Unknown*

Lesson #2

Another lesson my mother taught me was as a man I need to *always stay true to my word*. From an early age she instilled in me that as a man, a black man, all I have is my word. Once that is tarnished you are left with no intrinsic value, and a man with no value is worthless. From that point on, after her explaining to me the severity of keeping my word, I tried my best at all cost to abide by her wishes. Now don't get me wrong, extenuating circumstances will arise and I understand things do not always go as planned, but that is when as a man, you must step up and take responsibility for your actions.

> *"Be true to your work, your word, and your friend."*
> *- Henry David Thoreau*

Lesson #3

Never marry until you can allow your spouse to keep her whole check. My mother would explain to me that a woman should never have to feel the burden of being the primary income provider. I understand that is a very opinionated statement, but coming from my mother, it was as good as gold. Throughout my life, at times, I saw my mother struggling. I saw the tears in her eyes and the trust in her heart. It was times when all my mother could do was trust in God for a way to be made. I remember times being asleep in my room at night and my mother coming in to check on me. Once she noticed my eyes slightly beginning to open she would begin to speak. I could always tell that whatever she was about to say was something that had been on her heart for a while and she needed to get it off of her chest. A good majority of the time the talks we had late at night centered on how a man truly should treat a woman. I remember her telling me to be very observant of how our household was being run, and the stress that was being put on her. I made a promise to always support my family, spiritually, emotionally, and financially. So to my future wife, your check will be YOURS and my check will be OURS.

"A wife is the joy of a man's heart"

- Talmud

Lesson #4

Always be there for your family. Now that I am older and can understand things a little bit more clearly, I have come to the realization that my father's absence probably had more of an effect on my mother than it did me. My father's shortcomings forced my mother to not only head the maternal role but take the lead as the head of household, friend, coach, and even disciplinarian. These roles can become overbearing at times. As a child I just noticed the big picture, the final product. I didn't see the struggle and sacrifice that my mother had to endure just to see me smile at times. For all of her hard work I am forever grateful. My mother would always pull me to the side and point out a situation that my father was absent from and encourage me to do better and to always be there for my future children. She would explain to me that no child should be continuously let down and I should always remember how I am feeling now, so when I grew up and had my own family I would forever be not only sympathetic, but empathetic, to my children's needs.

> *"When you look at your life, the greatest happinesses are family happinesses."*
>
> *- Joyce Brothers*

Lesson #5

Always follow your dreams. Life is not about regrets. You must always follow your heart and your passion. The last thing you ever want is to be stuck in some mundane routine thinking about what could have been. I'll never forget my mother telling me, "Dalen, never let anyone tell you the sky is this limit. What do you think they made spaceships for?" Growing up with that type of rationale in the back of my mind, I knew I could do and accomplish anything I put my mind to, and I wasn't going to let anyone stop me. I truly appreciate my mother till this day for always supporting me in everything I said I wanted to do. I cannot honestly remember one time that my mother even subtly crushed a dream of mine. This woman is the type of mother that if I said I wanted to be a cowboy she would have done everything in her power to try and buy me a horse. I sincerely believe that having this strong support system truly molded me into the man I have grown into today.

> *"All men dream but not equally. Thos who dream by night in the dusty recesses of their minds wake in the day to find that it was vanity; but the dreamers of the day are dangerous men, for they may act their dream with open eyes to make it possible."*
>
> *- T.E. Lawrence*

Lesson #6

Never quit. Quitting is for losers and there is no future in it. My mother used to explain to me that as a man if I start something I must see it through. Galatians 6:9 says, *"And let us not be weary in well doing: for in due season we shall reap, if we faint not."* No matter what task I decided to embark on my mother always taught the importance of me seeing it through. Stick-to-itiveness is a tremendous quality that separates the good from the great, and she always let it be known that I was destined for greatness.

> *"Great works are performed not by strength but by perseverance."*
>
> *- Samuel Johnson*

Lesson #7

Always acknowledge God in everything you do. With my mother being a pastor I came from a strong religious background. From an early age my mother taught me the importance of having a strong relationship with my Heavenly Father. She would explain to me that without Him nothing is possible, and to always thank Him for the blessings you have as well as those you don't. I remember as far back as I can remember my mother reciting Proverbs 3:5-6 to me, *"Trust in the Lord with all thine heart; and lean not unto thine own understandings. In all thy ways acknowledge Him, and He shall direct thy path."* Till this day I still recite this verse both in my head and aloud when times get rough, it has gotten me through a lot of situations. Merely reciting this verse reaffirms my confidence when I am weary and downtrodden.

Lesson #8

Remember to inspire life into others. My mother always taught me to LOVE, LIVE, LIFE. She taught me to LOVE myself unconditionally, LIVE my life to the fullest, and to always inspire LIFE in others. For some reason this mantra is something I hold dear to my heart even to this day. Following these three simple commands will change your entire outlook on different situations. It allows for you to broaden your thought process and strengthen your character as an individual.

> *"One way to get the most out of life is to look upon it as an adventure"*
>
> *- William Feather*

Lesson #9

Be watchful of the things that come out of your mouth. You can always have what you say. This is a concept that I do not play around with or take for granted. I truly believe that the power of life and death lay on the tongue. This is a simple principle that comes from Biblical teachings, but have since then been mentioned in such books as *"The Secret."* It is amazing how your thoughts and your words can quickly become reality. My mother taught me from early on that whenever I felt the need to say something negative just replace it with something positive. Something that simple can change your whole outlook and motivation level. For instance, when it comes to money worries, instead of saying "I have never been this broke in my life," try instead "I have never been this RICH in my life!" It may seem like a joke and people may laugh, but as much as you reiterate these words it subconsciously becomes a part of your everyday thought process. Try it, it works wonders.

Lesson #10

Never become friends with two people who are already friends. This is a lesson I can honestly say that I have always paid close attention to because I have seen the negative outcome that could possibly come from it. The message behind this rule is simple; it speaks to loyalty. The point my mother was trying to make to me was very elementary at best. Her motive was to get me to understand that two established friends only have loyalty to one another, and any new outside entity is just that, an outside entity. She would tell always tell me a story of this guy she knew who had just graduated high school and gone off to college where he met two guys. The two guys were best friends and had grown up together. My mother went on to tell me that everyone who met the pair knew that something wasn't right. One day someone out of the trio came up with the bright idea to break into the car of someone in town. The two friends decided it would be best if they broke into the car while the other guy, the "outside entity," would hold the gun and remain lookout. Midway between the pair scavenging through the vehicle, the owner of the car must have woken up and heard the commotion. The door to the house swung open and there stood the disgruntled owner with a pistol in his hand. Not built for this lifestyle, scared out of his mind, and trying to protect his "friends," this young man fired two shots into the chest of the unsuspecting owner, killing him. Needless to say all three "friends" were quickly apprehended by the authorities. During the interrogation the "outside entity," with no prior criminal history, quickly found out whom his friends were not. His so called "friends," both of whom had past criminal records, told the police that it was all his idea and that he had a pistol and forced them to commit the crime. Needless to say, they both got away with light sentences and are out walking free today, while the "outsider" received life in prison with no chance of parole. I guess that's friendship for you. Being conscious of your surroundings and the people you associate yourself with could prove to be life altering at times, remember to always pay close attention.

Lesson #11

Always respect your elders. Respect was something taught in my household from an early age. Growing up around my grandmother and all women I was forced to learn how to respect not only women but the elderly as well. My grandmother was quick to let me know that she was not my equal and she demanded my respect. I laugh about it now, but my grandmother used to carry around a handheld billy club wrapped in black tape, and would threaten me with it if I ever acted up. That was enough for me. I knew not to cross her or any other elderly person. Besides the fear I had for her as a disciplinarian, was the respect I had for her because of the knowledge and wisdom she had and shared with our family daily. Knowing all the things she had been through and all the different things she had seen in her lifetime truly amazed me. Every time she opened her mouth it was like a journey through history. Through her, I truly understood the concept of deference and respecting those that came before me.

"A single conversation across the table with a wise man is worth a month's study of books."

- Chinese Proverb

Lesson #12

Always be slow to speak and quick to listen. In author Robert Greene's *The 48 Laws of Power* he boldly states, *"But the human tongue is a beast that few can master. It strains constantly to break out of its cage, and if it is not tamed, it will run wild and cause you grief. Power cannot accrue to those who squander their treasure of words." (pg. 33)* My mother would always tell me to not let my mouth get me in trouble. For me, that was about as easy as telling a determined two-year-old to not eat the candy sitting right in front of him while your back was turned. Just like any other hardheaded growing young boy, I had to learn the hard way. I found myself constantly in trouble for talking back and speaking out of turn. After whooping after whooping and punishment after punishment, this rule finally became a reality. It wasn't until later on in my life that I truly understood the value of listening, and how far something that simple could possibly take you. Trust me, learning this rule at an early age is an investment worth having.

Lesson #13

Remember to tithe and give God 10% of your income. Before someone starts to tithe I feel as though they should have a clear understanding behind what they are doing. Writer Ben Atkinson explains, "When you give your money to a higher purpose outside of yourself, you are showing God that you can be trusted with what is given to you. You also show God that you trust He will take care of your needs and you will not have to rely on material things." My mother broke down the purpose of tithing to me at an early age, and she made sure that I tithed off of every bit of money that came through my little hands. After tithing so long as a child, it became like second nature, and it is something that I don't even think twice about anymore. I have come to the realization that tithing 10% of my earnings is miniscule compared to the amount of blessings that God has bestowed upon me and my life over the years. To me, tithing the entire 100% of my earnings still wouldn't be enough.

Lesson #14

Always treat people the way you would like to be treated. This saying goes back to the beginning of time, and as elementary as it may sound, it still holds a lot of truth. Some people would explain this concept by using the term "karma," my mother on the other hand taught this principle by encouraging the importance of being an all-around genuine person. The way you treat a person is a direct reflection of how you subconsciously view yourself. If you are happy and content with yourself then that light will radiate out of you and into others.

> *"Thoughts lead on to purposes; purposes go forth in action; actions form habits; habits decide character; and character fixes our destiny."*
>
> *- Tryon Edwards*

Lesson #15

Always help when and if you can, and never be a part of anyone else's hurt and pain. People please understand that life is not always about YOU, but more so about the number of selfless acts you engage in that result in the blessing of others. The gratification that occurs when doing something kind for someone else, in my eyes, truly increases your own self worth. The reversal of this argument speaks on assisting with the hurt and pain of others, whether intentional or unintentional, constant negativity brings down your morale as well as the morale of others.

> *"The wise person understands that his own happiness must include the happiness of others."*
>
> *- Dennis Weaver*

Lesson #16

Always give more than what you expect to receive. The act of giving just to receive never sat well with my mother. She always taught me that giving should always be done with purest of intentions. The joy brought to someone else's life by a random act of kindness should be enough of a reward by any means. Someone once told me that giving comes from the heart, you are either a giver or a taker, and believe me a taker ALWAYS stands out in a crowd.

"A human being feels able and competent only so long as he is permitted to contribute as much or more than he has contributed to him."

-L. Ron Hubbard

Lesson #17

Never be afraid to ask for help. My mother used to always tell me, "The only dumb question is the one unasked." From an early age she taught me the importance of asking questions. She would explain to me that if I ever didn't know something or needed help with a task, that assistance was only a question away. My mother would further instruct me to never let my pride get in the way of a blessing, and to always be grounded enough to realize my shortcomings and humble enough to seek assistance.

"The strong individual is the one who asks for help when he needs it. Whether he has an abscess on his knee or in his soul."

- Rona Barrett

Lesson #18

Clothe yourself in humility and always check for pride.

"Many people believe that humility is the opposite of pride, when, in fact, it is a point of equilibrium. The opposite of pride is actually a lack of self esteem. A humble person is totally different from a person who cannot recognize and appreciate himself as part of this worlds' marvels."

- Rabino Nilton Bonder

Swiss psychiatrist and influential thinker Carl Gustav Jung once stated, "Through pride we are ever deceiving ourselves. But deep down below the surface of the average conscience a still, small voice says to us, something is out of tune." My mother would always preach to me the importance of not having pride. She would let me know time after time that pride could most certainly be the reason for someone's downfall. I remember being in elementary school and my mother telling me an old Aesop Fable about pride that involved two roosters. The story began with two roosters in fierce fighting with one another to become king of the farmyard. After a long violent battle, one rooster finally gained the upper hand and made the other surrender. Ashamed and humiliated, the losing rooster scurried away and hid in a quiet corner, while the boastful winner began to fly up to a high wall, flapping his wings rapidly and crowing of his victory as loud as his voice would carry. At this exact moment an eagle soaring by pounced on the unsuspecting rooster and carried him away in his talons. Watching from the distance, the losing rooster came out from his place of hiding and ruled the farmyard from that day forth. For some reason the symbolism in this fable still resonates with me till this day.

> *"A boastful winner is nowhere near as admirable as a graceful loser."*
>
> *- Dalen L. Spratt*

Lesson #19

Travel as much as you can. Traveling is an excellent source of experience. English writer G.K. Chesterton once proclaimed, "The traveler sees what he sees, the tourist sees what he has come to see." I can honestly say from as long as I can remember my mother has been a huge advocate of traveling. Every chance she had she was finding a way to get me out of Dallas. I really didn't understand the significance of traveling until my older years. I sit back now and look at old pictures from past trips and wish that I had paid more attention to my surroundings and had done a lot more in these settings. Over the years I have done a lot of traveling and met a lot of unique people, but the two excursions that stand out the most in my mind are my trips to Europe and Asia. By engulfing myself into these foreign cultures I was forced to quickly adapt and learn, and I loved every minute of it. Before my trip to Asia, I ran across a quote from Anglo-French writer Hilaire Belloc stating, "I have wandered all my life, and I have traveled; the difference between the two is this – we wander for distraction, but we travel for fulfillment." A life without travel is truly one left unfulfilled.

Lesson #20

Reach for the stars and settle for the moon. This was just my mother's way of telling me that anything was possible, and to not let anyone tell me anything different. One day while reading, I ran across a passage by an unknown author that stated:

> *"Through pain find strength*
> *Through birth find healing*
> *It is never easy to keep reaching for dreams*
> *Strength and courage can sometimes be lonely*
> *friends ---*
> *But those that reach the stars, walk in stardust."*

Lesson #21

Always remember 2 Corinthians 5:7 and walk by faith and not by sight. While growing up, my mother would always preach the importance of faith to me. Even at a young age, whenever it came down to me really wanting something to be done, no matter how kiddy it was, she would recite a quote by Patrick Overter:

"When you have come to the edge of all the light you know
And are about to step off into the darkness of the unknown,
Faith is knowing that one of two things will happen:
There will be something solid to stand on
Or you will be taught how to fly."

I loved that quote so much that I quickly committed it to my memory, and cannot wait to pass it along to my children one day, to keep them motivated and encouraged.

Lesson #22

Always let the word of God be your last source. While growing up, it would always amaze me how people would question the word of God. I could not for the life of me fathom how someone could question what came out of the Bible, a book written by a higher being, but would take Webster and his dictionary as the end all and be all. You have never once heard anyone question the validity of a definition found in the Webster Dictionary, a book written by man. Man leaves room for error and inconsistencies, God does not. Whenever you are in a time of need and things seem hopeless always look to God and his word, the answer will always be there.

Lesson #23

Never underestimate your enemy. This lesson is one that everyone should pay close attention to. Underestimating or giving your enemy too much credit can prove to be very detrimental, and cost you everything. Prime example, while filming the television show *I Want to Work for Diddy Season 2* I was placed into a household with nine other contestants all vying for the same prize, a position at Bad Boy Entertainment. I worked my way down to the final 4 where I thought I had an alliance with the only two remaining female contestants. After weeks of planning, they led me to believe that we were going to set up Dan, the remaining male contestant other than myself, to go home, and then we three would battle it out fair and square with one another. At the last moment of elimination all three contestants turned their back on me, the strongest player, and voted me out. I was so shocked at the moment that all I could do was smile. I had underestimated my opponents, and thought that we actually shared some type of mutual understanding. I am just grateful that I learned that experience in a truly non hostile environment. There have been many others who had to learn the same lesson the hard way, ending in their demise.

> *"Underestimating is like letting a wolf in your farm. Never underestimate and definitely don't be too overconfident for you will be arrogant and ignorant. When we view ourselves too highly and others too lightly, destruction occurs."*
>
> *- David Kam*

Lesson #24

Never let anyone tell you what you can or cannot do. My mother would always explain to me that my life was in my hands and I had to live it for myself and no one else. There are only two people that have control of your destiny, and that is God and yourself. In this world there are a lot of people who just genuinely do not like to see others become successful. You must use these people and their negative attitudes as your fuel and motivation to power you to success.

> *"People become really quite remarkable when they start thinking that they can do things. When they believe in themselves they have the first secret of success."*
>
> *- Norman Vincent Peale*

Lesson #25

Reputation is what people think, Character is what you are. Growing up, my mother would always recite to me an old American Proverb that stated, "If you take care of your character, your reputation will take care of itself." Dictionary.com explains character as being the aggregate of features and traits that form the individual nature of some person or thing.

> "His reputation is what men say he is. That can be damaged; but reputation is for time, character is for eternity."
> - John B. Gough

I learned at an early age that ones' character could easily be judged by the way he treats the people that can do absolutely nothing for him. Treating the janitor just as you would treat the president not only speaks volumes about you as an individual, it simultaneously transmits a sense of encouragement and positivity into lives of others.

Lesson #26

There are no free rides in life, eventually we must all pay. This was basically my mother's way of explaining to me the importance of hard work. She would go on to tell me that anything worth having is worth working for. I sincerely took her words to heart, and apply them to everything I do in life. It seems that with me the harder I work for something, the larger the payout. It is like a get a sense of fulfillment and gratification to see something that I worked extremely hard for come into fruition.

> "When you live for a strong purpose, then hard work isn't an option. It's a necessity."
> - Steve Pavlina

Lesson #27

A man should always be head of his household and should always take care of his family. This is a lesson that my mother truly held dear to her heart. There were too many times while growing up that I saw the disdain in my mothers' face from having the burden of being the head of the household dropped on her shoulders because her counterpart was not pulling his weight. That was a look that I always knew I did not want to ever see on my future wife's beautiful face. My mother would explain to me that it is a man's responsibility to provide for his family at all costs. After speaking to a few different men and women, the aggregate consensus of the bunch was, a man that does not try to provide for his family is worthless. The last thing we need in our society today is an abundance of worthless men. That is a trait that must be broken. Young men should be trained from an early age the importance of providing and carrying the weight of not only themselves, but their families alike. This is a concept that has been brought down for ages, but has seemed to skip certain generations. We as men need to stand up and become the change that we so enthusiastically speak of.

Lesson #28

Make more friends than enemies. This lesson is very simple and straight to the point. Although life is not about pleasing others, it is always better to have a group of people for you than having them against you. With that being said, being cordial and appropriate at all costs will make this dream turn into a reality.

> *"Give us grace and strength to forebear and to persevere. Give us courage and gaiety and the quiet mind, spare to us our friends, soften to us our enemies."*
> - Robert Louis Stevenson

Part 7 – Gwen
An Unexpected Ending

Today is March 17, 2010, one day before Dalen's 25th birthday. I completed my part of this book nearly five months ago… so I thought. It's funny how life has a way of carrying you back to your past without any help from you.

My life has literally spiraled out of control. That uninvited guest came knocking at our door, and for whatever reason, my husband allowed it to come in and once again set up residence. The two of them embraced each other like father and son, like mother and daughter, making the relationship between the two more powerful now than ever before. My only peace in all of this now is that Dalen is not here on a daily basis. He doesn't have to see and hear all of the ugliness that is being displayed in our home, in front of anyone who happens to be here.

I want to believe all of this is a nightmare and I'm in a deep sleep. When I wake up, I'll find everything the way it was a few months ago, yet I know I am not dreaming.

I called Dalen everyday to ask him if he was finished with his part of the book. I always got the same answer, "no Mama, I'm still working on it." I shared Dalen's inability to finish his part of the book with a friend of mine. Her reply was a strange one to me. She said, "Maybe the story isn't complete yet which is why he can't complete his part." I had no idea what she meant, but time would answer all questions. She was right; the story is not complete, and I don't know how or when it will be. All I do know is that everything and all things eventually come to an end. It's what happens in between the start and the end that is really important.

I am standing directly in the "in-between." Some days I don't know if I'm coming or going, and now it is to the point where I can't even talk to my husband anymore. He doesn't want to hear anything I have to say and frankly, I don't want to hear anything he has either.

The past has a way of repeating itself. I am still trying to figure out how that old uninvited guest was allowed to re-enter my husband's life. As I sit in bed writing, my mind is perplexed. I have prayed so many times trying to get an answer to my question, and at this point, I have received no answers. Maybe I am missing something; perhaps the answer began to unfold over two years ago.

On December 27, 2007, my husband went in for a colonoscopy. I thought it would be uneventful and without problems because I had had one only a few years earlier. When I woke up, the doctor was standing over me, telling me everything was fine and there were no problems, and that he would see me in five years unless I began to experience unforeseen problems.

I was so wrong when it came to my husband. When his procedure was over and I was allowed to go back and be with him, he was still a little drowsy. The doctor came out and motioned for me to come toward him. As I walked toward him, fear gripped me. I could tell from his posture that something wasn't right. He looked at me and said, "Gwen, I'm sorry, it's cancer." My knees buckled and the doctor had to catch me to keep me from falling to the floor.

He gently placed me in a chair and asked if I was okay. With tears rolling down my face, I told him I would be fine. Boy, how I'd lied. I was not fine, okay, or any other synonym that described a state of well being. As a matter of fact, I was everything but fine. All I could think about was how I was going to tell my husband and his poor mother this devastating news. Spratt's father and grandfather both died from colon cancer. His mother is a breast cancer survivor. On my side of the family, my sister Faye, the matchmaker for Spratt and me had died of bone cancer a few years earlier. This was a cycle I was becoming to know too well.

As I sat in that chair, cancer and death were all I could see. With Gods help, I finally pulled myself together enough to walk over, along with the doctor, to my husband's bed. While we both stood there looking at him, Dr. Young informed Spratt that he had cancer. I had to fight back the tears, but to my surprise Spratt took the cancer news better than I thought he would. He responded as though he had been told he had a bad case of the flu and nothing more. I listened very carefully as Dr. Young told us what our next steps would entail. We were told he would have to take several rounds of radiation and chemotherapy.

After we listened to everything the doctor had to tell us, we thought Spratt would be back to work in six or seven months. We are now into the third year that my husband has been out of work. We have gone through three surgeries, radiation and chemotherapy, and a colostomy bag that I had to learn how to put on him and empty properly… the whole nine yards. It was an experience I will never forget and pray I will never have to go through again. The scripture, "I can do all things through Christ Jesus who strengthens me" really came alive in me. Truly Jesus Himself had to give me the strength to go through this ordeal and to continue to go through it.

The only thing I can contribute my husband's relapsing to is the constant stress he has been under for nearly three years. I must admit the stress has been unbearable, however, he had begun to do so well I really started to believe we had finally gotten over this period in our lives. We had even talked about him teaming up with a more mature counselor in AA and starting a 12-step program at our church. He was really excited about being a part of the program and eventually leading the group himself.

Because of everything that is going on in my life at this point in time, I can't seem to see the forest for the trees. Dalen is aware of his father's problem. I couldn't hide it from him this time around even though I wanted to. Circumstances wouldn't allow it. While Dalen was visiting home for a few days his father just suddenly left, and was gone for nearly two days. Of course Dalen caught on, and I knew he was eventually going to ask where his father was.

I was downstairs sitting in my office reading the word of God. I looked up and saw Dalen slowly walking down the stairs. Our eyes met and that old familiar question came out of his mouth, "Mama, where is Daddy?" I couldn't lie or pretend he was some place he wasn't. I couldn't pretend that he had come and gone again because Dalen had been home most of the time himself, going in and out of our bedroom. As I looked at Dalen, I could see the little boy who always asked that question. For a second, I was transported back to the past. I felt so helpless and so angry at my husband for putting me in a position that would cause me to be the source of Dalen's hurt and disappointment.

I quickly snapped back and told Dalen that his father had gotten back on drugs. I can't even describe the look that came across Dalen's face. At that point, if I could have taken those words of truth back, I would have and might even have told the biggest lie to keep from hurting and disappointing him any more than he already was.

Dalen stared at me with his beautiful brown eyes and the words that came out of his mouth shocked me. He asked, "How do you know, Mama, are you sure?" I could tell from the question he asked that he didn't want to believe it. His father had done so well. When I told him I was sure, Dalen walked back up the stairs and didn't come back down anymore that day. He didn't even bother to eat anything. I decided the best thing to do was to leave Dalen to himself and allow him time to process the news he had been told.

Several times throughout the day I tried to will myself to walk up those stairs and check on Dalen. My heart wanted to but my head kept telling me to leave him to himself and give him time to deal with it before he would have to see his father face-to-face.

As I stated earlier, my life has spiraled out of control since December 28, 2007. Things were going so well for me and my family. God had answered so many prayers for us. We moved into our dream home in May, 2007. God blessed me to decorate my whole house. I didn't have to wait on anything except for the furniture to be delivered. Everything was going so great. It was like a fairy tale. Spratt, Dalen and I had life by the tail and we were not letting go. The dreadful big "C" news on December 28, 2007 forced us to unexpectedly let the tail of life go.

Since so many things went wrong the last couples of years that would lend themselves to my husband's relapse, I simply don't know where to begin. When we bought our house, we were doing well financially. Money was the least of our problems. We had done well with our investments, our stocks were doing great, we had CDs, bonds, a savings account and I even had what my sister called "Mad Money." Mad money is money that is kept at home. It's all cash that you can get to anytime you need it. Only Dalen and I knew the location of that Mad Money which was usually $40,000 - $50,000 dollars. We had medical insurance so I anticipated no problems. Wrong again!

The day finally came for the first surgery which cost nearly $75,000 along with a nine day hospital stay. Our insurance paid for the surgery but then there were radiation and chemotherapy treatments. Unexpectedly, I received a letter from the insurance carrier informing us that the cancer was pre-existing and they would not pay for the chemo or radiation treatments. Those treatments totaled over $100,000.00 and we had to pay out of pocket. Of course the house note, car note, insurance, etc. still had to be paid. Soon after, there was a second and third surgery that the insurance carrier refused to pay, so we had to come out of pocket once again. Eventually our money began to run out. We ran behind with everything: house, car, credit cards, etc. Spratt was unable to go back to work because of the surgeries so he applied for disability and of course, he was denied. He had absolutely no money coming in. My income from the church was our only source of income. There were times the church could not pay me so there would be no money coming in at all. Friends and family helped as much as they could, but our overhead was just too much for them to carry us.

We were left with one choice: bankruptcy. It was a very hard decision and one we said we would never make. Life has a way of making you do those things you said you would never do. I believe the filing of bankruptcy might have been the one thing that started nagging at Spratt's spirit because it was something he never wanted to do.

Over the last three years, there hasn't been any money for a family vacation, no Christmas gifts and no birthday gifts. I think Spratt began to feel pressured. He tried his hands at a couple of things to bring income into the house, but things didn't pan out for him. He would have to ask me for money to buy something as small as a hamburger. That didn't help at all. It didn't make him feel good about himself. He would talk about how bad he felt and being unable to take care of his family. This is a man who in spite of his addiction had always taken very good care of us. I worked because I wanted to, not because I had to. Then everything changed so fast that I couldn't pinpoint the day or time. It was like one day everything was fine, I went to bed and the next morning all hell had broken loose.

All of Spratt's old behaviors started coming back; not coming home and not answering his cell phone. Everything and I mean everything is so out of control I don't know what to do or where to turn. I feel so alone in this battle that doesn't seem to have an ending. I try very hard not to involve Dalen in my troubles. I want him to be free to live his own life. I don't want him to worry about me and what's happening with me.

Every since I was a little girl, I had always kept a journal. I was taught as a child that writing down my thoughts and experiences could not only be therapeutic but they could possibly come in handy one day. Although I finished writing what I thought was the end of my part of the book roughly five months ago, I continued to write in my journal. Instead of summing up the days, I've decided to add excerpts from my personal journal detailing my thoughts of the instances that took place after my husband's relapse.

Today is April 21, 2010, and Spratt is supposed to leave tonight for Jackson, Mississippi to enter into a drug rehabilitation facility that I had made plans for him to attend. Because of our financial situation, we could not afford a plush rehab facility. The insurance company would not pay for him to attend so we had to pay out of pocket. Because we were paying out of pocket, I had to choose a facility that was good but affordable. When I had done all I could do for my husband, I decided I needed a break from him and he needed one from me, so I began to make phone calls to various rehab facilities. The one in Mississippi was the most affordable and I felt it had the best program for my husband. The program ranges anywhere from six weeks to nine months. It is my hope he will stay the entire nine months.

Today is Saturday, April 24, 2010. Not to my surprise, Spratt did not come home to go to Mississippi. The last few days have been very stressful for me. I tried calling him on his cell but naturally it was turned off. I had no idea where to begin looking for him. He no longer went to his old place of business. He was gone from Sunday night to Thursday night. When he came home on Thursday the only question I asked was whether or not he had forgotten he was to go to Mississippi. He simply replied, "Time got away from me." I, in turn, had no reply for that million dollar answer.

Spratt went into our bathroom and took a thirty minute shower. When he came out he went to bed. Within a few minutes he was asleep, making all kinds of noises. I knew those noises were coming from that drug demon and I couldn't bear to hear it all night, especially since I hadn't slept in three or four nights. Now that I knew he was okay, I wanted to sleep myself. My body had knots all over it due to his absence. Finally, I couldn't take those loud, strange noises anymore so I called his name over and over until he finally answered me. I asked him to please sleep in one of the other bedrooms. Of course he was offended, but for the life of me I didn't care. I was offended he had been gone so long and missed his appointment in Mississippi. He got up and stormed out of the bedroom to sleep in another room. He was too upset with me to sleep in the bedroom downstairs, so he went upstairs where he wouldn't have to be close to me and could be as far away as possible. Frankly, I wanted him to be as far away from me as possible. I didn't want to be awakened out of my sleep by him or his strange noises.

Monday, April 26, 2010, I could hardly wait for the rehab facility in Mississippi to open so that I could call and see if they still had room for him. I had called on Thursday morning to inform them that Spratt didn't come home and asked them how long they would hold his bed. The lady I spoke with politely informed me they didn't hold beds because they were already very crowded. I immediately started to pray for God's favor. I knew only God could hold a bed for Spratt.

When I called on Monday morning and told them who I was and what I wanted, the person I spoke with told me everyone was in a staff meeting and that she would speak with the counselors as soon as they were finished. She said she would call me back within thirty minutes. I waited for over two hours and she never returned my call. I became very nervous. I prayed and then called her back. The Lord blessed me to talk with the nice lady I had originally spoken with at the beginning of this ordeal. Her voice was very warm and gentle and I could tell from the warmth in her voice that she cared about the families of the rehab patients. I could tell she felt my pain and heard the desperation in my voice. In addition, she remembered me and knew just who I was.

When I told her my problem, she asked me to let her talk with the counselors and that she would call me back within thirty minutes. She actually called back! When I answered the phone and heard her voice, I could tell God had given me favor. I knew they were going to take Spratt. She told me they would process Spratt in on Friday, April 30 at 11:00 a.m. I was happy but very disappointed. I wanted her to tell me to have Spratt there on Tuesday morning. I didn't want to wait but I had no choice. God had answered my prayer and I didn't want to push it with the rehab staff.

A couple of hours after me solidifying Spratt's plans to enter rehab again, he walked into the kitchen to get something to eat. I quickly followed behind him to let him know that I had spoken with the rehab facility and that they would take him on this coming Thursday. He yelled at me and told me not to talk to him that way. For a weak second, I became very angry, the nerve of him yelling at me, as if I had done something wrong. The anger left as fast as it came. I knew it wasn't him talking to me, it was the drug demon. He stayed away from me all day Monday. I was very happy he decided to keep his distance. I had the bedroom to myself; I didn't have to share the television; I didn't have to cook and I didn't have to make small conversation. I was totally free and had a wonderful day with the downstairs all to myself.

He even told me he wanted to go to rehab so he wouldn't have to be around me. Naturally I came back with, "and I want to get away from you too. I need a break!" I think that statement really angered him. If looks could kill, I would have died an instant death. We stayed away from each other all day and night Monday. I had a wonderful night's sleep. It rained all night long. It wasn't heavy but a light steady rain that lends itself to a peaceful sleep.

On Tuesday morning, Spratt was downstairs and in the bedroom bright and early. His whole disposition had changed. He was happy to see me and began talking as if nothing had happened. I played the game along with him. I didn't want to irritate him. I wanted him to remain calm and keep his mind on going to Mississippi. It's now Tuesday evening. I cooked dinner and we watched television together. We even laughed together. As I write, he is in the kitchen eating again. He has been eating all day and I couldn't believe one person could hold so much food.

Tomorrow is Wednesday and he leaves Thursday night at 11:05 p.m. I decided not to drive him to Mississippi. It would be too hard on both of us. Wednesday is going to be a very big day. I don't want to give him any reason to get upset with me and leave home. I know his mouth is saying he will go, but I really don't know if it is in his heart. He is fast asleep. I pray he will sleep the entire time and not get up and leave in the middle of the night while I am asleep, as he has done many times before.

Well, today is Wednesday. We made it through the night without his leaving. If we can make it through today, I know he will be on the big Greyhound bus tomorrow night.

Once I get Spratt to rehab, I will be able to relax for a minute and then begin to deal with all the other unresolved issues that I need to deal with…mainly the house. We received a letter a couple of days ago telling us the bankruptcy had been dismissed and the house was no longer protected and that the mortgage company was free to pursue foreclosure again. At this time, I am so tired I can only handle one thing at a time. Of all the issues that I am facing, my husband's deliverance is number one on my list. If we lose the house, we can always get another one someday. We can always rebuild our credit, but I can never get the husband that is inside this shell of a man back unless he is free of drugs. You simply cannot share life with someone for nearly thirty years and not care about them and want them to be free and enjoy all that life has to offer.

Today is May 9th and my husband has been gone almost two weeks. On May 10th, I spoke with both him and his counselor. His counselor reports that he is doing well with no problems, so far. My husband reports that he is adjusting fine. He is eating and sleeping okay.

I have been home alone for these two weeks praying and talking to God about everything that is going on in my life and seeking His wisdom for my situation. The only word I have clearly heard from Him is, "God is in control of all my circumstances." Knowing that God is in control gives me the courage to keep going. If I didn't think God was in control, I would not have the courage or strength to see this trial all the way through.

Another week has passed. I have spoken with Spratt a couple more times. He sounds as if he is in a really good place. The laughter was back in his voice. I wish I could say the laughter was back in my voice because I love to laugh and tease. I look forward to the days ahead when my laughter will be uncontrollable. Until then, I will pray and hope for the best.

PART 8 – DALEN
Does Cancer Change Anything?

The clock had just struck midnight bringing in the New Year 2008, and I found myself amongst friends and family at my mother's church. This was nothing new to me because my mother used to always say to me, wherever and however you brought in the New Year would have a direct effect on the remaining 364 days. So, if you wanted a blessed year, what better place to celebrate than the church. After all the Happy New Year's had rang out, and hugs were passed around, I was approached by my cousin Kendra, the same cousin who had a major hand in my upbringing. Her exact words were, "How are you feeling about the whole situation?" I responded with a slight grin of confusion. I think she could tell by the look on my face that I had absolutely no clue what she was talking about. She then responded with, "You don't know?" What was once a grin of confusion quickly turned into a stare of worry and anticipation. I responded with, "What are you talking about?" She would not tell me. She told me that I needed to speak with my mother, that it would be best if I heard it from her. At that exact moment in what seemed like an eternity, my mind was running a mile a minute. Every negative thought that you could possibly imagine was running loose through my mind. My mind raced from one thought to the next. I went from thinking about my mother being terminally ill to my parents divorcing.

In all actuality what seemed like an 8 hour conversation between me and my cousin was only about 30 seconds. As I was sitting there thinking the worse, out of the corner of my eye I could see my mother walking toward me getting ready to greet me with a humongous Happy

New Years hug. Before she could reach me with her arms spread wide I spoke up abruptly, "What is Kendra talking about? I need to speak with you." My mother then responded with, "I'll talk to you about it when we get home." For me, being the type of person that cannot stand when someone starts to tell me something then stops, that answer was not good enough. I persisted and insisted that she tell me whatever needed to be said right then. After a pause that seemed to last an eternity she began to explain to me how my father had been diagnosed with cancer.

I don't quite know how the average person would take hearing that one of their parents had been diagnosed with a potentially life threatening illness, but I know my emotions. In a disturbing way I was just relieved that the bad news was not centered on my mother. Since my relationship with my father had been a rocky one, I could not for the life of me seem to be able to muster up any type of compassion. In my heart I honestly felt that time had just caught up with him and whatever happened was destined to be. Although my thoughts seemed very harsh, it was the reality of the situation and our relationship. It seemed as if my only concern was how my mother was going to be affected by the situation, and I rapidly found out. The next few years proved to be very trying for my mother. The cancer did something to my father that drugs never did; it fully disabled him. Because of the chemotherapy and other treatments my father became deathly ill and couldn't work anymore. This caused a huge problem. This forced my mother to have to use her one income to support a lifestyle that had been sustained by the salary of an excellent medical doctor. This alone tried my mother's faith severely.

My father's battle with cancer ended with him being victorious, but the damage had been done. With my father out of work so long and my mother having had to stretch herself even more thin, the tension in our home came back stronger than ever. We all hoped and believed that after my father survived cancer that he would see the importance in living, be grateful for a second chance and clean up his lifestyle. Boy were we wrong. As soon as he had fully recovered he went right back to his old ways, and once again it was just me and my mother, like always.

The Apology

I have been dealing with my father and our relationship my entire life. We have yelled, screamed, and almost come to blows. Through all of this I know deep down in his heart my father knew he had a problem and so desperately wanted to be forgiven by not only his family, but by himself as well. After I found out about my father's past and his current state, it was only discussed by me and my mother from then on out. My father and I never seemed to acknowledge his problems with one another. It was like the elephant in the corner that everyone sees but no one speaks about. I would sit and wonder to myself if he would ever come and speak to me about his drug addiction and his lack of parenting abilities. I felt that as his son, I needed an explanation, furthermore, an apology. Just like with my earlier experiences with my father, I knew not to hold my breath when waiting on either. I just could not for the life of me understand why he would not just come to me as a man and tell me his side of the story. I felt that he, at the least, owed me some kind of explanation.

It is kind of funny the way things work out sometimes. It was not until a few months after my mother and I decided to start writing this book that the opportunity to speak with my father finally presented itself. When my mother first approached me with the idea of putting our story on paper, I was a tad bit reluctant. I was not sure how I felt about divulging my families' secrets to the world. Another thought that crossed my mind was how my father would take reading about all the feelings and emotions I had been holding in the past 24 years. Still, after months of writing, he never once spoke to me about me and my mother's project. It was not until one Sunday morning on the way to church that he told me he needed to speak with me. As those words rolled out of my father's mouth the last thought in my mind was him apologizing. This was at a time in my life when I had just came back home to Dallas from filming a television show in New York and I was packing to move back to Atlanta. In my heart I just figured he was going to give me the usual "be careful out there" speech. As I was driving I looked over at my father as he was starting to speak again and I remember the look on his face being very distant. It was as if whatever he was about to say to me, had to be pulled up from out of the deepest part of his soul. As he began to speak I could not only hear, but feel, the emotions in his words. At that exact moment, in my eyes, this man went from being considered solely as my mothers' husband to me looking at him ever so briefly as my father. He began to tell me that he knew he was never much of a father to me and how much he regretted not being a major role player in my life. For some reason I kind of felt sorry for him. All the anger I had before then seemed to kind of wash away at that precise moment. He then explained to me how his father, my grandfather, was never there for him, never hugged him, never showed him any type of parental affection. With that being said it was as if I had a serene moment of clarity. Everything in my whole life, each conversation, each argument, each fight, suddenly made sense. Forget the drugs. Forget the alcohol. This was a vicious cycle of abandonment past down from father to son for the past few generations that needed to be broken immediately in this family. I had always said before that I would be nothing like my father when it came to raising my children, but at that exact moment I meant it with everything in my soul. Something had to be done. This cycle had to be stopped at me. I'd be damned if I continued this male corruption in my family. I was determined to be that change that my family so desperately needed. He then began to tell me that he sincerely apologized for not being there for me like he knew he should have been while I was growing up. He told me he was proud of the man that I grew up into and he just prays that it's not too late to build a relationship with me. I didn't speak, but amidst the silence was a mutual understanding and agreement. Although he didn't speak on his drug addiction, I knew the point he was trying to get across. Instead of me being vindictive and forcing an explanation I just accepted this conversation for what it was and left it alone. I figured it took him 24 years to journey this far to talk to me, whenever he was ready to say more he knew where to find me.

After it was all said and done, I felt relieved. I felt like the Bank of Dalen had finally relieved my father of his debt. Now that he had apologized and I accepted, I felt like I couldn't hold it over his head anymore, nor could I keep dwelling on it. For me to successfully accept his apology I had to forgive and forget and move on. I realized how could God forgive me of any of my wrong doings if I couldn't even forgive my father of his. Matthew 6:14-15 says, *"For if ye forgive men their trespasses, your heavenly Father will also forgive you: But if ye forgive not men their trespasses, neither will your Father forgive your trespasses."* I actually matured a little bit, and became that much closer to my father that day.

Part 9 – Letters

Gwen

To end our book, Dalen and I each decided to write a letter to Spratt telling him how we feel about his drug addiction and how it has affected the both of us. Hopefully, it will set all of us free.

Dear Spratt, my husband and the father of my son,

I really don't know where to start, but I can tell you that every word you read will be from my heart. My life with you has made me the woman I am today; a woman who loves God and family; a woman who has lived a single life even though we have been married the last twenty nine years of our lives together. I can remorsefully say, your drug addiction stole our youth from our marriage.

When I use the word "youth," I mean the young years; the years we could have gotten to really know each other; the years we could have grown together as a family with you being the head guiding us spiritually and physically.

I often ask myself if I would remarry you if I had to do it again. I want to say, "No, no!" But I also believe without you, I wouldn't be the mother of the best twenty-five year old black man in America today. I can definitely say this; if I had to do it over, I would not stay in this situation for twenty nine years. I would make an early exit with my son in tow. I would look for a man who was strong enough to choose Dalen and me over drugs or anything else that would cause alienation between us.

My husband, your addiction has caused me many sleepless nights. They could name a new river with all the tears I have shed. Your drug problem caused me to stop living and start to merely exist. At first I was so ashamed and embarrassed being married to a drug addict. I couldn't think; it was as if I was walking down a long dark road with no light in sight. I stumbled many times on that long, dark road, but thanks be to God, I never fell.

Your chosen life style forced me to become mother and father to our son, leaving very little time for myself. I should really thank you for that because as a result of it, Dalen and I are so very close to each other. We have a wonderful mother-son relationship. He often tells me I am his best friend. My husband, on the other hand, your drug problem has caused me to live a lonely life.

You gave Dalen and me everything we wanted, but you never gave us what we needed…your presence. When you chose to give us your presence, in most cases, your body was there but we still didn't have you. You would be in a deep sleep, so deep as a matter of fact that a bomb exploding in the room wouldn't have awakened you.

Spratt, I know deep inside you there is a true love for Dalen and me but your love for drugs overshadows your love for us. For that, I forgive you. I hold nothing in my heart for you but love. The word of God says, "Love bears all things, believes all things, hopes all things, love never fails." The word of God also says, "Love covers a multitude of sins."

My love for you has allowed me to bear this burden with you and for you for the last twenty nine years. Some people think I am the weakest and silliest woman in the world to have stayed with you this long., but like God, I hate divorce.

The intent of this letter is not to hurt you but to allow you to see into my soul the depth of hurt and pain your drug problem has caused me. I want you to see the depth of my love for you and my hope and desire to see you drug-free. I want to see you become the man God destined you to be.

P.S., I have not and will not give up on you. It's till death do us part.

Your wife,

Gwen

Dalen

Dear Lorenzo,

I call you Lorenzo not out of disrespect, but as approaching you now, man to man. There are so many things I wanted to tell you over the years that I just held back. Now that I am 25 years old, a grown man living my own life, I feel the need to get a few things off of my chest. I know reading this book may be hard for you and you may find out a host of emotions and feelings you probably never knew I had in regards to you, and that is something I will never apologize for. I grew up thinking you just didn't like me, I mean I know now what the reason was that caused these attitudes and mood swings but growing up I was truly oblivious to the fact. My whole life I carried resentment towards you. Unlike most children in regards to their fathers, I never looked up to you. You were never my role model. The only thing you were consistent in doing with me was letting me down, so much that I became immune to the way you treated me.

Writing my story opened up a lot of emotions that I never knew I had. Throughout the course of writing this book I have almost came to tears on more than one occasion, but I'm grateful. I am truly thankful that I was able to get these thoughts out in the open. I feel relieved and stress free. This writing has truly become very therapeutic for me. I say all of that to say, amidst all of the writing, I've done even more thinking. And I must say father, man to man, I apologize for the lack of respect that I showed you growing up until now. Despite your issues, you are still my father and I owed you more reverence than I ever showed you.

I honestly do not feel like I did my part to help your situation. I should have manned up and talked to you about your addiction. Instead of harboring ill emotions I should have been man enough to talk it out with you. Holding in these feelings was probably the worst mistake I have ever made in my life. And for that I sincerely apologize. I know you have done your wrong doings, but who hasn't. The Bible says we all have sinned and fell short of the glory of God, so who am I to judge you. Society has done that enough, so why have your family members add insult to injury?

Honestly, I am grateful to have you as a father. Even though you weren't around a lot, your absence did teach me how I should treat my family one day. By seeing what I missed out with you, trust and believe, I know how to step up to the plate for your future grandson/ granddaughter. So, indirectly, you actually taught me more than you probably would ever imagine. And for that I am grateful.

It kind of sucks that the manly things that a father is supposed to teach his son, I had to learn on my own, like tying a necktie, shaving, or even talking to the ladies, but as I sit and think, you and I did share plenty of good times. I sit back and laugh sometimes when think about you teaching me how to get waves in my hair, and me piling sport and wave in my hair and you cutting one of Mama's stockings just to make me a wave cap. I chuckle to myself when I think about the year you took me to Cancun for spring break and you took me to my first real club. I'd never in my life had that much fun. I remember when we went scuba diving that one time, and I thought I was about to drown. I bring up all these memories to say, thank you. Forget all the bad that has happened between us, I just want to thank you for all the GREAT things you were there for. Truthfully, I wouldn't trade you for the world. Without you and Momma I definitely wouldn't be the man I am today.

So from this day forth I promise to become that support system that we never were for one another. Let's let the past stay in the past and start a new beginning. I love you pops and I will always be here for you, no matter what.

Love Always…
Your SON,
Dalen Lorenzo Spratt

CPSIA information can be obtained at www.ICGtesting.com
Printed in the USA
LVOW131320260313

326121LV00001B/6/P